GW01220376

THE GREAT ALL-ROUNDERS

By the same author

Pelham Cricket Year, I – III
Benson and Hedges Cricket Year, I – V
The Wisden Book of Cricket Quotations
Summer of Success
Great One-Day Cricket Matches
'Tich' Freeman
Johnny Won't Hit Today
Percy Chapman
The Great Wicket-Keepers
The Book of One-Day Internationals
Ken McEwan
Cricket Heroes (General Editor)
A Walk to the Wicket (with Ted Dexter)
Cricket Reflections (with Ken Kelly)

THE GREAT ALL-ROUNDERS

David Lemmon

The Crowood Press

First published in 1987 by
The Crowood Press
Ramsbury, Marlborough,
Wiltshire SN8 2HE

© David Lemmon 1987

All rights reserved. No part of this publication may be reproduced or transmitted in any form or by any means, electronic or mechanical, including photocopying, recording, or any information storage and retrieval system without permission in writing from the publishers.

British Library Cataloguing in Publication Data
Lemmon, David
The great all-rounders.
1. Cricket players   2. Cricket – History
I. Title
796.35'8'0922   GV913

ISBN 0 946284 89 X

Acknowledgements
On occasions throughout the text the author has turned to *Wisden* for reference and contemporary report and has quoted from this source.

Picture Credits
All-Sport Photographic Ltd: pages 4, 9, 26, 37, 41, 52, 53, 56, 69, 105, 109, 115, 117, 121, 133, 136, 142, 149, 161, 167, 175.
BBC Hulton Picture Library: page 128.
Ken Kelly: pages 46, 60, 80, 97.
London News Agency: page 92.

Typeset by Chippendale Type, Otley, West Yorkshire
Printed in Great Britain at The University Printing House, Oxford.

In memory of my father who gave me my first sight of Constantine, Hammond, Miller and many others, for which I remain grateful.

CONTENTS

1 The Yardstick 1
2 Interregnum 17
3 The W. G. Grace of Australia 23
4 The Yorkshire Connection 35
5 The Golden Age of the County All-Rounder 51
6 Barnacle and the English Renaissance 73
7 Miller and his Disciple 88
8 West Indian Knights 104
9 The New Breed 113
10 Thwarted Genius 126
11 The Nottinghamshire Duo 139
12 Eastern Stars 153
13 Both! 171

1

THE YARDSTICK

Cricket records began with W.G. Grace. He first played for the Gentlemen against the Players at the age of 16. At the age of 18 he scored 224 not out for England against Surrey at The Oval and was dubbed 'the Champion'. He shared a record partnership for the first wicket at the age of 20, and at the age of 22 he became the first batsman to reach two thousand runs in a season. In 1876 he hit 344 for M.C.C. against Kent at Canterbury, the first triple century in the history of first-class cricket, and in the following week he played innings of 177 and 318 not out for Gloucestershire against Nottinghamshire and Yorkshire. Four years after these achievements, he was to score England's first Test century.

On 14 August 1874, on the second day of the match between Gloucestershire and Yorkshire at the College Ground, Clifton, he took the wickets of Smith, Ulyett, Thewlis, Greenwood and Mr J.L. Byrom at a personal cost of 44 runs. As Grace took five or more wickets in an innings on 240 occasions during his illustrious career, it may seem strange to draw particular attention to this match at Clifton when the Champion scored 127 and took 5 for 77 in the second innings, and a Yorkshire side, reduced to ten men by illness, was beaten by an innings. The significance of his five first innings wickets, however, is that they took his total number of victims for the season to 104. Two weeks earlier, at Bramall Lane, Sheffield, he had scored 167 for Gloucestershire against Yorkshire and, in doing so, had passed one thousand runs for the season. That match, for the benefit of Luke Greenwood, had also seen Gloucestershire victorious by an innings with Grace taking 11 wickets. He ended the season with 1,664 runs and 140 wickets from the twenty-one matches in which he had played. It was the first time in the history of the game that a cricketer had reached the landmarks of a hundred wickets and a thousand runs in the same season, and a new word, the 'double', entered the vocabulary of cricket.

Grace was to repeat the achievement in the next four seasons, establishing another record in 1876 when he took 129 wickets and scored

2,622 runs. He had erected a standard of greatness against which all future cricketers who aspired to be known as all-rounders would be measured.

It would be wrong to suggest, however, that William Gilbert Grace was the first all-rounder in the history of the game. In 1832, in the pages of *The Examiner*, John Nyren recalled the cricketers of his time, among them his father, Richard, landlord of the Bat and Ball Inn, the only building close to Broad Halfpenny Down where the men of Hambledon established their famous club in the second half of the eighteenth century.

Richard Nyren was the major figure in the Hambledon Club: 'the chosen General of all the matches, ordering and directing the whole', and was 'a good face-to-face, unflinching, uncompromising, independent man'. His son proudly asserted that he never saw 'a finer specimen of the thoroughbred old English yeoman'. He was a left-handed bowler with a high delivery, that is he bowled underarm, but with a force, subtlety and variation in point of delivery that made it somewhat distant from the style that we usually associate with that term. It was said that 'his balls were provokingly deceitful'. He was a safe batsman and an excellent hitter, and, although rather a stout man of medium height, he was extremely active in the field.

The same height as Richard Nyren, equally active, but slimmer, was William Beldham, 'Silver Billy', the last survivor of the famous cricketers of the Hambledon era. He got this nickname from his handsome fair hair and complexion and his intelligent features. He was considered by John Nyren to be the finest batsman of his day. He was safe, hit the ball remarkably hard and was one of the first batsmen to be spoken of as giving an aesthetic pleasure by his style. 'It was the beau-ideal of grace, animation and concentrated energy.' He was a fine fielder in any position, and he bowled a brisk, underarm medium pace. It was in his bowling that his intelligence was most apparent, for he was a noted assessor of batsmen's weaknesses and exploited them.

There was an exuberance in Beldham's life which typifies the all-rounder. He played his last important match when he was 55 and lived until he had turned 96. He had an appetite for cricket and for life that was never satiated. He excited exuberance in others. The Reverend John Mitford, editor of *The Gentleman's Magazine*, was unstinting in his praise:

'Never was such a player! so safe, so brilliant, so quick, so circumspect; so able in counsel, so active in the field; in deliberation so judicious, in execution so tremendous. It mattered not to him who bowled, or how he bowled, fast or slow, high or low, straight or bias; away flew the ball from his bat, like an eagle on the wing. It was a study for Phidias to see

Beldham rise to strike; the grandeur of the attitude, the settled composure of the look, the piercing lightning of the eye, the rapid glance of the bat, were electrical. Men's hearts throbbed within them, their cheeks turned pale and red. Michael Angelo should have painted him.'

If Mitford was a champion and enthusiast for Beldham, then William Denison, the first cricket reporter, was a most fervent admirer of Alfred Mynn, unquestionably the greatest all-rounder in the quarter of a century before the arrival of W.G. Grace. Denison considered Mynn 'one of nature's finest specimens – he stands 6 feet 1 inch in height, and weighs 18 stone; sometimes a few pounds over and at others a few pounds below that standard, and is withal gifted with extraordinary activity'. He was 'one of the brilliant wonders of his day'.

Alfred Mynn was the lion of Kent. He was born at Goudhurst in 1807. His family were yeoman farmers noted for their stature and looks. He moved to Harrietsham when he was 18 and first appeared for the Gentlemen at Lord's in 1832. He played for Kent from 1834 until 1859, and was also one of William Clarke's original All England Eleven in 1846. He was a hard-hitting middle order batsman and a right-hand fast round-arm bowler. It was considered one of the finest sights in cricket to see Mynn advance and deliver the ball, and it was as a bowler that he made the deepest impression.

What made Mynn so fine a bowler was that he combined great pace with great accuracy in a manner that was unapproached at the time. He had begun as a rather wild fast bowler with a long run and very little control, but was persuaded to cut down his run to six paces. His run-up was steady and controlled and his splendid physique enabled him to generate genuine speed off his six paces.

To his fearsome speed and power as a bowler, Mynn allied his strength as an attacking batsman. In 1836 he made 283 runs for twice out in two consecutive matches, a feat that was unapproached by any other batsman at that time. A gentleness of manner and a transparent honesty of nature were combined with his strength and prowess as a cricketer. He trained on beef and beer, and every night he took to bed with him his old family prayer-book and a tankard of ale in case he should wake up thirsty. He had an abundance of spirit, energy and courage which, as we shall see, characterises the great all-rounder.

In 1836 Mynn scored 45 not out and 92 for M.C.C. against Sussex at Brighton, and he also took 9 wickets in the match. A few days later he played for the South against the North at Leicester. At practice he hit a ball hard on to his right ankle which began to swell so much that it was

Alfred Mynn. 'One of the brilliant wonders of his day.' 'The greatest match-winner the game produced before the advent of W. G. Grace.'

doubtful as to whether or not he would be able to play. Rain on the first day meant that he did not have to take the field until the second when, batting with a runner, he scored 21 not out. Unwisely, he decided to bowl and field, with the result that even walking became difficult and very painful, for the ankle had continued to swell.

The game, sparked by a Nottingham boast to Leicester, had attracted great attention and some five thousand people had attended on the first day's play. Mynn was unwilling to withdraw from a match to which so much importance was attached, even though his whole leg was now swollen and the pain had increased. He insisted on batting on the third day and limped to the wicket when the score was 91 for 3. He batted for just under five hours, did not give a chance and hit 125 not out as 223 runs were scored while he was at the wicket. He was opposed by Redgate, the only man of the time comparable to Mynn in pace, but Redgate reflected: 'it mattered not what length I bowled him – the better I bowled, the harder he hit me away.'

Lord Frederick Beauclerk, himself a noted all-rounder, and in his zest, prowess and confidence in his own ability a worthy predecessor of W.G. Grace, came to meet Mynn and congratulate him when he returned to the tent. His Lordship was appalled by the sight of Mynn's leg, so swollen and inflamed that it seemed impossible that the man could stand, let alone bat for nearly five hours. Lord Frederick at once sent for his carriage and arranged that Mynn should be put on the stage-coach which was leaving Leicester for London.

When Mynn was taken to the stage-coach it was discovered that because of his huge frame and with his leg stiffening, it was impossible for him to be seated inside. The only alternative was to hoist him on to the top of the carriage where the luggage was usually strapped and to lay him flat on the roof. In this manner he was brought to London. He could go no further and was laid up at a tavern in St Martin's Lane, where doctors debated whether limb or even life could be saved. He was then taken to St Bartholomew's Hospital and the leg was saved, although it was nearly two years before he was to play cricket again.

He played his last game in May 1861 when he was 54, for Southgate with his friends the Walkers, against Upton Park in Essex. In October of the same year, he died of diabetes.

Alfred Mynn was loved by all. Never before, and arguably only W.G. Grace since, had a cricketer commanded such universal respect and admiration. He was the greatest sporting personality of his day, and his presence on any ground was sure to increase the attendance by a substantial margin. He was a mighty hitter, a fast bowler and a magnificent fielder in the slips where his massive hands took catches lost to others. He had all the qualities necessary for the great all-rounder. 'All were proud of him, all loved him!' His epitaph passed into cricket literature and folklore: 'Lightly rest the turf upon thee, kind and manly Alfred Mynn!'

Perhaps Mynn's greatest impact upon the game had been made in his appearances for the Gentlemen against the Players. The famous fixture had first been played in 1806, but by 1840 the match was in jeopardy, so dominant had the professionals become.

Mynn first played for the Gentlemen in 1832 when the Players won by an innings and 34 runs, but from 1842 to 1849 he was to dominate the fixture. The Gentlemen won five and lost three of the matches played in that time, and Mynn took 56 wickets and scored 298 runs in them. His last match for the Gentlemen was in 1852, and in his twenty-one appearances for the amateurs he scored 605 runs and took 107 wickets. After one more victory, in 1853, the Gentlemen did not win again until 1865. Alfred Mynn was the greatest match-winner the game produced before the advent of W.G. Grace.

When the Gentlemen met the Players at The Oval in 1865 they included in their ranks for the first time William Gilbert Grace. He was two weeks short of his 17th birthday, a lanky lad of 6 feet in height. He was in the side primarily for his bowling and made a good start, taking 4 for 65 in the first innings and 3 for 60 in the second. Batting at number eight, he scored 23 and 12 not out, but the Gentlemen were beaten by 118 runs. A week later, in the return match at Lord's, he opened the batting with his elder brother, Edward Mills Grace, an outstanding all-rounder in his own right, and scored 34 in the second innings as the Gentlemen won by 8 wickets.

W.G. Grace was to play for the Gentlemen against the Players for another forty-one years, and he bestrode these matches like a colossus. The size of his influence upon the games can be seen from the fact that before his arrival the Gentlemen had won only 14 of 59 meetings. In the 85 matches in which Grace played, the Gentlemen were victorious on 39 occasions with 17 matches drawn. He contributed more than six thousand runs and took 271 wickets in these matches. His last appearance for the Gentlemen was at The Oval on 18 July 1906 when, on his 58th birthday, he scored 74. The match was drawn.

As he grew older Grace battled against increasing bulk, but his ability did not diminish. Indeed, in 1895, his 47th year, he set new records as a batsman. On 16 and 17 May he hit 288 for Gloucestershire against Somerset at Bristol. He batted for 320 minutes, hit 38 fours and did not give any chances. It was the hundredth hundred of his career. In the ninety-one years since, only twenty other batsmen have equalled this proud record and they all played more matches on far better wickets.

A week after his hundredth hundred, Grace led Gloucestershire against Kent at the Bat and Ball Ground, Gravesend. Kent batted into the second day and reached 470. Gloucestershire replied with a score of 443, of which Grace made 257. He opened the innings and was last man out just before lunch on the last day. Kent were then bowled out for 76, leaving Gloucestershire to make 104 in 75 minutes to win the match. They reached their target, for the loss of Wrathall, in 60 minutes, Grace hitting 11 fours in his 73 not out. It was the most remarkable game of the season and caused a great stir, but there was an event of greater significance a week later when the Champion hit 169 against Middlesex at Lord's and, in doing so, passed a thousand runs before the end of May. He played 10 innings during the month and scored 1,016 runs, average 112·88. Only two other batsmen, Hammond and Hallows, have scored a thousand runs in May, and four others, Hayward, Bradman (twice), Bill Edrich and Glenn Turner have reached a thousand runs before the beginning of June.

There was so much public excitement at Grace's achievements – his hundred hundreds, his thousand runs in May, and his feat at Gravesend when he was on the field for the entire match – that a National Testimonial was organised. The *Daily Telegraph* collected £5,000 by means of a shilling subscription, and the M.C.C. collected £2,377 2s, less £21 18s 10d expenses. Grace was entertained at banquets in both London and Bristol.

It was not the first time that Grace had received public acclaim. In 1879, on the second day of the match at Lord's between Over 30 and Under 30, he was presented in front of the Pavilion with a National Testimonial in the form of a clock and a cheque for £1,458. The match itself was to have been for the benefit of Grace, but he suggested that it should be for the benefit of Alfred Shaw whose match earlier in the season had been ruined by bad weather.

In every sense, W.G. Grace was a national hero. People today who know nothing of cricket recognise his picture and his name, for he transcended the game itself. His face was as famous as Queen Victoria's, and his image was everywhere, even engraved on the legs of tables in public houses. He was the best-known Englishman of his time, and C.L.R. James rightly castigates the historians G.M. Trevelyan, Raymond

Postgate and G.D.H. Cole who presumed to write social histories and failed to mention Grace.

Grace came into the game when it was primarily a provincial pursuit dominated by professionals intent on taking what they could from it. When he left it, cricket was an expression of popular life, woven into the very fabric of the nation. He had tamed the professional fast bowlers, who before his arrival had swept all aside, and reshaped the game with the force of his own personality and the magnitude of his ability.

Grace was the son of a Somerset doctor who had a large practice and lived in Downend, a quiet village four miles from Bristol. Dr Henry Mills Grace had married Martha Pocock, and they had five sons, of whom W.G. was the fourth. The parents bequeathed to their children enthusiasm of the highest order. The father believed that it was wise to superintend boys' games as carefully as their lessons, and he gave them every opportunity to develop their talents. He laid out a pitch in one of the orchards in the grounds of their house, 'Chestnuts', and the boys played at every conceivable moment. Even the family dogs were trained to retrieve cricket balls.

'I cannot remember when I began to play cricket,' wrote W.G., 'Respect for the truth prevents me from saying I played the year of my existence, but I have little hesitation in declaring that I handled bat and ball before the end of my second.'

The family rose at dawn in order to play a few hours of cricket before work or study. They organised clubs and played matches all over Gloucestershire, and W.G. took part in these games from the age of nine onwards. Martha Grace was as much a driving force as her husband. She watched every ball, preserved newspaper cuttings of the reports of important matches and took great care of score books. Her brother was a keen cricketer and gave W.G. much help.

W.G. himself was adamant that he was not a born cricketer, for he believed that cricketers were made by coaching and practice, but he agreed that he was born 'in the atmosphere of cricket'. 'My father, who was a keen sportsman, was full of enthusiasm for the game, while my mother took even more interest in all that concerned cricket and cricketers.' Grace was gifted with a fine physique, but even that was developed by the healthy, active, outdoor life that he lived as a boy.

His progress was quick and consistent. He first appeared at Lord's in 1864 when he scored 50 and 2 and took a wicket for South Wales against M.C.C. and Ground. The following year he made his debut for the Gentlemen against the Players, and thereafter he reshaped cricket and

W. G. Grace. 'He played cricket with the whole man of him in full action, body, soul, heart and wits.'

created the record books. The 54,896 runs, 126 centuries and 2,864 wickets are testimony to the man's ability, but they tell us nothing of the style or of the man himself, and we will find in both characteristics which have been common to the greatest all-rounders.

Grace was a big man, full of gusto. He quickly filled out from the lanky stripling of 17, chosen for the Gentlemen for his medium pace bowling, to the massive, bearded figure recognised by all. There was authority in his demeanour. For such a big man he was remarkably nimble on his feet, and it is worth noting C.B. Fry's remark that none of the English cricketers could waltz like W.G.

From the beginning, his approach to the game was positive. He did not believe that the game should be played in silence, and his high-pitched voice was often heard on the field in comment or exhortation. He played vigorously and with humour. His vitality was inexhaustible, and his stamina and enthusiasm unsurpassed. No day was too hot for him, or too long. It is recorded that even in his later years, he was known to have spent the night at the bedside of a patient and to have gone out the next day and scored 200 on the Clifton College Ground.

His batting revealed his zest for cricket and for life. He is quoted as saying that games were not won by leaving the ball alone, and that he hated defensive strokes because he could only score three off them. His bat was unerringly straight and his back-lift high. He came down quickly on the 'shooters' of his day and combined the soundest defence with violent attack. His hitting was powerful, his placing unequalled. He tended to eschew dainty shots like glances, taking more delight in feeling the bat hit the ball hard. He was too big a man for subtlety. None before him had ever driven so powerfully or so fruitfully on the on-side, yet, by his own admission, he did not indulge in the pull until he was turned forty. That he did indulge in it then can be verified by the comments of another great all-rounder, Wilfred Rhodes, who encountered Grace when he was near the end of his great career. 'He would take a good length ball from outside his off-stump and bang it over mid-on's head like a cannon ball.'

Grace's batting philosophy was simple: he went out at the ball to score runs. No man or woman ever dozed when he was batting.

His prowess as a batsman has tended to obscure his greatness as a bowler. In his early days, he bowled medium pace with a purely round-arm action, but he reduced his speed at about the time that he first completed the 'double'. He moved the ball in from leg, but relied mainly on his total command of length and direction, and on his ability to probe for a batsman's weakness and to exploit it quickly. In his bowling he was a great thinker, and his field placings and bowling to his field were as scientific as anything that has been seen since.

One of his favourite ploys was to lure batsmen to destruction by feeding them an apparently gentle full toss on the leg stump which would end up in the hands of deep square leg. In the first years at Gloucestershire, Fred Grace caught many batsmen in that position. Edgar Grace, W.G.'s nephew, remembered how, in a childhood forty years past, W.G. 'when bowling his slow round-arm with his short shuffling run, he would often change the position of his deep square leg a few yards and the batsman would hit his next ball straight into his hands.'

There were many contemporaries who asserted that if Grace had not been such a wonderful batsman, he would have been the best slow bowler in England. As it was, only Alfred Shaw and Southerton could match him, and the first signs of decline in his bowling did not come until 1892 when he was 44 years old. Yet ten years later, for M.C.C. against the Australians, a very strong side, he turned in a remarkable performance which left Pelham Warner in raptures. 'Of all the feats I witnessed by W.G., the one that most surprised me was a bowling one. It was in 1902 – he was then nearly 54 – against the Australians when Trumper was at his very best. The Old Man took the ball and I thought we were in for it. Instead the Australians were – 5 for 29; marvellously baffling, too, not a pinch of luck to help an analysis of which Tom Richardson would have been proud.'

As befits the great all-rounder, W.G. was an outstanding fielder. At first he fielded in the deep and was noted for his mighty throw, but as the years passed he moved to point where he was surpassed only by his brother E.M. In the autumn of his career, he found bending a little difficult.

Grace's talents were not confined to the cricket field. He was an admirable runner, rider and shot, and – lest we should forget – he was a student of medicine. Indeed, when *Vanity Fair* pictured Grace as the first cricketer among its 2,387 cartoons in 1877, naming him simply 'Cricket', it said of him that he intended to devote himself in future to medicine and would play only for Gloucestershire and M.C.C. He had just passed his examinations as a surgeon at Edinburgh and thought it best to follow the examples of his elder brothers by settling down to the busy life of a general practitioner and gradually retiring from cricket, but his plans were changed by the arrival in England of the first Australian side in 1878. Grace did, for many years, hold a parish appointment as a doctor in Bristol, with a locum doing his work in the summer.

Grace was in poor form at the beginning of 1878. He captained M.C.C. against the Australians at Lord's in May and was out for 4 and 0, bowled by Spofforth in the second innings. Spofforth took 11 for 20 in the match which was over in a day, the Australians winning by ten wickets. This was the stimulation he needed. He led the Gentlemen of England to an innings victory over the tourists at Prince's less than a month later, top-scoring with 25 and taking 6 for 52 in the match.

The Australian challenge presented Grace with another world to conquer. He played under Lord Harris when England beat Australia at The Oval in 1880, the first Test match in England. Grace scored England's first Test hundred (152), shared the first century partnership in Test cricket with A.P. Lucas and took three wickets in the match. His last Test match came nineteen years later when he led England in a drawn match against the old enemy at Trent Bridge. It was the first of a five-match series, the first occasion that five Tests had been played in England, and the first Test to be played in Nottingham. The great man scored 28 and 1 and bowled 22 overs for 37 runs without taking a wicket. He was 50 years, 320 days old when the game ended. Only one man, Wilfred Rhodes, has ever played for England at a greater age, and he made his Test debut in Grace's last Test.

It had not been intended that this should be his last, and C.B. Fry holds himself responsible for bringing the Champion's Test career to a close. They gathered for a Sunday lunch in order to select the side for the second Test, and Fry was a little late arriving. When he arrived, Grace thrust a question at him before he could sit down, the answer to which had to be yes or no. 'Do you think that Archie MacLaren ought to play in the next Test match?' Fry was of the opinion that MacLaren should play, for he had been most successful in Australia the previous winter, and unhesitatingly replied 'Yes, I do'. 'That settles it,' said Grace.

What Fry had not realised was that he had been asked to give a casting vote, and that the point at issue was whether or not the old man should resign from the England eleven. When this became apparent to Fry he tried to make other suggestions, but the Champion, and the others, were adamant. Fry was saddened, because it was Grace's belief in his ability that had led to his own inclusion in the England side and now he was responsible for the ending of Grace's career of cricket for England.

It is interesting to note in Fry's autobiography, *Life Worth Living*, that he considered that Grace, in 1899, was a greater name in cricket than Don Bradman was in 1938, and that he was as good a slow bowler at the age of 51 as Clarrie Grimmet, Australia's leading leg-spinner, was in the 1930s.

Grace believed that the time had come for him to retire from Test cricket because he could no longer move about in the field or run his runs as he had been able to at one time. Grace was positive in all he did, and for one who had been a natural athlete, a quarter-miler and a hurdler, limitations in the field could not be accepted.

He was a very kind man, devoted to his wife, hearty, but totally aware of his own position in society and in relation to the game of cricket which he had, in fact, created, or at least reshaped. 'Except for his real friends, W.G. had a formidable eye and a beetling brow; he had the merry heart of the full-blooded English yeoman type, but he knew who he was and who you were, and he possessed, when it came to it, an Olympian dignity.'

His kindness was obvious in his treatment of young players. James Gilman was told to report to Crystal Palace in June 1900 to play for Grace's London County team against the West Indian side. Young and inexperienced, Gilman was sitting nervously in the dressing-room, surrounded by famous players, when Grace approached him. 'Are you nervous?' he asked, his eyes twinkling. Gilman admitted that he was terrified.

Grace went out to toss up, and when he came back he told Gilman to put his pads on because he was opening the innings with him. 'It was a kind and very shrewd move, because he could see I'd have been reduced to a jelly if I'd had to wait to bat. It was typical of W.G. – his bark was worse than his bite.' Grace and Gilman put on 136 for the first wicket, and the great man was out shortly after lunch.

'That wasn't at all surprising,' Gilman recalled. 'The "Old Man" was very keen on the catering and we had a sumptuous lunch, with hock and claret on the table. He had a real whack of the roast, followed by a big lump of cheese. He also tackled his whisky and seltzer, which was always his drink.'

Grace was large in bulk, and large in character and action. He was not autocratic, but he stood no nonsense and suffered neither fools nor slackness of any sort. There were those who believed that he imposed his will on umpires and even that he cheated, but his actions were motivated by the belief, and the correct one, that the crowd had come to see him play. Indeed, on occasions the admission price was increased if he were playing.

Had Grace played today, he would have become a sporting millionaire, a star of gigantic proportions. As it was, 'he did not do too badly for an amateur'. That Grace had a concern for money is undeniable. His friend, C.E. Green, was the man who motivated Essex towards first-class cricket. Green invited Grace to stay with him for the opening match of importance at Leyton, kept him some days afterwards and gave him the use of one of his finest greys (Green was master of the Essex hunt). When he had left, Grace wrote Green a warm letter of thanks, adding that he would like to receive twenty guineas for the advertisement he had afforded the new ground at Leyton. Green sent the cheque, but he was angered and saddened by the request.

There is, perhaps, in all greatness an attendant sense of vulnerability which creates the need to provide for an uncertain future. Grace has not been the only cricketer to have such a deep concern for finance while facing the threat of bleak years beyond cricket.

Finance loomed large in Grace's life. In 1896 there was a strike by the England professionals who had been selected for the match against Australia at The Oval. Their grievance was that the amount that they received was inadequate, and it was implied that the 'amateurs' received large sums of money for playing. The Surrey Club was moved to issue an official statement in which it was set down that Grace had never received more than ten pounds a match to cover his expenses from the West Country and his three or four day stay in London. The statement served to make many feel that Grace was not getting sufficient out of the game to meet his immediate expenses. He was concerned about money, but he was not mercenary.

It is likely, however, that financial considerations played some part in his break with Gloucestershire. It was rumoured in 1899 that he had been invited to become manager of the new cricket ground at Crystal Palace and captain of the London County Club then being formed. He had lost his beloved daughter at the end of 1898 and spent much time with his wife, not wanting her to be alone at the time of their great loss. Unwisely and with a total lack of diplomacy, the Gloucestershire committee tried to force him to make his intentions clear midway through 1899, and Grace resigned the captaincy of the county he had helped to create on 28 May. He left with 'the greatest affection for the county of my birth, but for the Committee as a body, the greatest contempt'.

In the early days, the Gloucestershire matches had been like a family party. 'Like other families they had their little differences, but there was a great feeling of comradeship among them, and they played cricket with tremendous zest.'

Grace's obituary in *Wisden*, a splendid piece of writing by Sydney Pardon, commented wisely on the Crystal Palace venture. It 'did not add to his fame. He was in his 51st year when he left Bristol, the experiment being made far too late. Many pleasant matches were played at The Palace, but they were carried through in too leisurely a spirit to appeal to a public brought up on cricket of a much sterner character. If tried 15 years earlier the project might have proved a success. As it was the London County faded out when Mr Grace's contract with the Crystal Palace Company came to an end.'

That end came in 1904 when Grace hit his 126th and last first-class hundred, against M.C.C. and Ground. In the next four years he was to play another twenty-seven first-class matches. In 1906, at 58 years old, he scored 241 runs, average 26·77, and took 13 wickets at 20·61 runs apiece. His final first-class match came at The Oval on Monday, Tuesday and Wednesday, 20, 21 and 22 April 1908. On the first day, Easter Monday, The Oval was covered with snow, and the match was played in bitterly cold weather. Grace was bowled by Busher for 15 and for 25. He bowled 2 overs for 5 runs. Grace played his last match for M.C.C. against Old Charlton, at Charlton, on 26 June 1913. He scored 18, but he did not bowl.

Grace was amateur in spirit, but totally professional in application. He always wanted to be part of the game, and he wanted to win. Perrin, the Essex amateur, told how in his first game for the Gentlemen he had scored 17 in his first innings. Grace told him: 'You're going in first with me next time, young'un. Now be sure to have very long nails put into your boots, and take care to run up and down the pitch to ruin it. That is our only chance of winning the match. They would be suspicious of me, but they would never dream of you as new in cricket being up to such tricks.' The story was related by Home Gordon, and it is likely that it is apocryphal, but if such stories have grown, it is because the Champion had such an unquenchable appetite for participating and succeeding. He was not just a great batsman who could bowl or a bowler who was a good batsman; he was a great all-rounder, one who was of Test match quality as both batsman and bowler. There have been none to equal him, and very few have approached him.

Grace died at Fairmount, Eltham, in Kent, on 23 October 1915, and amid the carnage of the First World War England paused, shocked, for one of the greatest of men had passed from the scene. At the end, he had been horrified and perplexed by the slaughter of a generation of young men, for his own days had been life-enhancing.

Frederick Gale, the cricket historian, told how, at the time when Grace was establishing himself as the greatest of all cricketers, an old man brought him a pair of pads as a present. The donor said that the pads had belonged to Alfred Mynn and that Grace was the only man worthy to wear them.

In 1986 Frank Keating wrote a book on Ian Botham in which he forwarded the England all-rounder's claims to be considered the greatest all-rounder in cricket history. However, Keating himself voiced the belief that Grace's ghost would challenge this most strongly, and that Ian Botham might have to settle for second greatest.

W.G. Grace remains unassailable. He is the cricketer against whom all others must be measured. Cardus wrote of him that he was bound to be loved for he was so happy in his play. He played cricket with 'the whole man of him in full action, body, soul, heart and wits'.

'His nature was always alert, his spirits agile.' He dwarfs those who came before and those who have come after him. No other cricketer has stood so symbolically for the game itself, or has done so much to further it.

2

INTERREGNUM

It is something of a surprise that it was a great amateur who was the first to achieve the 'double' and set standards for future all-rounders. In the evolution of cricket in the nineteenth century the amateurs were batsmen, gentlemen who employed professionals as bowlers, but often these professionals, like Diver, Fenner and Wisden, were most competent batsmen and brought strength and prestige to country house teams. Wisden, at The Auberies in North Essex, was responsible for I Zingari crashing to defeat in 1848, and that league of gentlemen was one of the few associations to resist the temptation to strengthen its ranks by signing a professional bowler.

In 1870 James Southerton took 210 wickets with his round-arm off-breaks for Surrey, and Alfred Shaw took 201 wickets in 1878, but the great Notts bowler and Southerton (whose son became editor of *Wisden*) could not be ranked as batsmen with Grace. The Champion matched these two professionals with his bowling and obliterated them with his batting. He took 191 wickets in 1875, and 179 in 1877, and in each of those seasons scored nearly 1,500 runs, which was a meagre aggregate for him. He accomplished the 'double' seven times and stood supreme.

Surprisingly, the only all-rounder to approach Grace in the earlier days was another amateur, A.G. Steel, and the first player to accomplish the 'double' after Grace in 1882 was C.T. Studd, who was very much an amateur and a gentleman.

Alan Gibson Steel was a schoolboy phenomenon, being outstanding at Marlborough. He won his blue as a Freshman in 1878, when he topped both the batting and bowling averages of a side which won all its matches and beat the Australians by an innings. Steel's contribution to that epic victory was an innings of 59 run out and match figures of 5 for 106.

He was four years in the Cambridge side and was captain in 1880. Short, strong, quick on his feet, Steel was an attacking batsman with a wide range of shots, but it was his slow bowling, with a total command of the leg-break, which was his greatest strength. He hit eight first-class hundreds, including two in Tests, and only two men, Goonesena and

Napier, have taken more wickets than his 198 in their years at Cambridge.

In 1878, for Cambridge, the Gentlemen and Lancashire, he took 164 wickets, but his work as a barrister prevented him from playing regularly after he left university, so he was never able to develop his talents to rival the greatest all-rounder in cricketing history.

The same could be said of Charles Thomas Studd, a character who would not have been out of place in *Chariots of Fire*. C.T. Studd was the most famous of three brothers, all of whom played for Eton, Cambridge and Middlesex. He was a batsman in the classic mould, upright in style and strong on the off-side. By the time he went up to Cambridge in 1880, he was considered to be among the best batsmen in England.

The following year his renown increased, and at the end of the season he played in the Scarborough Festival. In the second match he took 6 for 31 and 6 for 43 to bowl I Zingari to a 159-run victory over Yorkshire. He was fit, strong and powerful, and in his years at Cambridge he was to take 130 wickets at 16·30 runs apiece with his very brisk medium pace, delivered with a high action.

Studd was seen as the natural successor to Grace when, in 1882, still short of his 22nd birthday, he swept all before for Cambridge and Middlesex, hitting 1,249 runs and taking 131 wickets. He had a triumph in the Varsity match as Cambridge won by 7 wickets. He took 7 for 54 and 2 for 48, and, opening in the second innings, hit 69 out of 146, being out when only 2 runs were needed for victory. His half-brother, George Brown, captained the eleven and hit 120 in the first innings. C.T. was to be captain in 1883, and John Edward Kynaston Studd, an elder brother, destined to be Lord Mayor of London in 1929, led the Cambridge side in 1884.

Surpassing Studd's performance in the Varsity match were his performances for Cambridge and for M.C.C. against the Australians under Murdoch in 1882. They were reckoned to be one of the strongest bowling sides ever to visit England, with Spofforth, Palmer, Garrett, Giffen and Boyle, but Studd hit 118 and 17 not out as Cambridge beat the tourists by 6 wickets. He also took 5 for 64 and 3 for 106 in the match. Six weeks later he scored 114 and took 4 for 26 as M.C.C. drew with the Australians at Lord's.

Studd continued his outstanding success when he appeared for Middlesex in August of the same year. His batting average for the county was 23 and he took 58 wickets at 14 runs each, including twice claiming Grace at Cheltenham for 9 and 0 as Middlesex won by 8 wickets. Yet the season was to end ingloriously for C.T. Studd.

When England met Australia at The Oval on 28 and 29 August, in the only Test match of the summer, Studd was an automatic selection. He was not called upon to bowl in the first innings as Peate and Barlow shot out Australia for 63. Studd became one of the demon Spofforth's victims as the Australian fast bowler took 4 wickets for 2 runs in his last 11 overs to restrict England to a first innings lead of 38. Studd, at number six, was bowled for 0.

Studd made his first contribution to Test cricket when he caught Bannerman in Australia's second innings and bowled 4 overs for 9 runs. England were left to make 85 to win. Studd was dropped down to number ten. When he came to the wicket England were 10 runs short of victory. Spofforth had taken 14 wickets in the match, but Studd had taken two centuries off the Australian bowling in the summer, so surely he would be able to conjure up the 10 runs required. The tension was great, and during the dramatic final stages of the match one spectator died of a heart attack and another gnawed through the handle of his umbrella.

Studd gave his own account of the events. 'The weather was cold. We sat in the Committee Room, and the windows were shut because of the cold. Except that such strange things happen in cricket, none dreamed we should be beaten.

'We had made over fifty for two wickets (there were less than ninety required to win when our innings began); everything was over, as they say, bar the shouting; runs had come freely enough. Then came the time when the best English batsmen played over after over and never made a run. If I remember right, something like eighteen to twenty overs were bowled without a run, maiden after maiden. They got out, and Hornby on his own account began to alter the order of going in. He asked me if I minded and I said, "No." Then things began to change and a procession began. Of course Hornby told me he was holding me in reserve. So I went in eighth and saw two wickets fall and myself never received a ball.'

Boyle took the 2 remaining wickets and Australia won by 7 runs. Peate, the number eleven, who was no batsman, had been told to leave the run-getting to Studd and to take care, but he hit a two, lashed out at a straight ball from Boyle and was bowled.

It was this defeat which provoked the mock obituary in *The Sporting Times* to the effect that the body of English cricket would be cremated and the ashes taken to Australia.

Studd was in Ivo Bligh's side that won two and lost two Tests in Australia the following winter, but he contributed little. He was never to play Test cricket again.

Studd had been top of the first-class batting averages in 1882 with 1,249 runs, average 32·86, and he was second in 1883 when he averaged 41·13 for his 1,193 runs. His 112 wickets meant that he again completed the 'double', and in that season was joined by the first professional to achieve the feat, Wilfred Flowers of Nottinghamshire.

The *Cricketing Annual* said of Studd that he must be considered the leading all-round player in England: 'For the second year in succession he must be accorded the premier position as an all-round cricketer, and some years have elapsed since the post has been filled by a player so excellent in all the three departments of the game.'

He came down from Cambridge after a career that was described as 'one long blaze of cricketing glory'.

Studd began the 1884 season in splendid form, hitting 141 not out to take M.C.C. to victory over Kent at Lord's. Against the Australians a week later he took 6 for 96 and 1 for 33, as M.C.C. won by an innings. He appeared in very few matches for Middlesex, but for the Gentlemen of England he took 4 for 69 and 1 for 61 as they too beat the Australians. The Gentlemen were beaten by Cambridge University, but Studd had match figures of 13 for 147.

On 26 June 1884 Charles Studd appeared for the Gentlemen of England against the Australians at The Oval. He took the wicket of Giffen and, opening with Grace, was out for 10. In the second innings he took the wicket of Boyle, and on the last day, again opening with Grace, he made 23 in a first wicket stand of 60. On 28 June 1884 he left the field at The Oval and first-class cricket for good. He was heir apparent to Grace, and he was 23 years, 178 days old. The cricket world stood before him, for he is still ranked as one who could have been among the very greatest all-rounders that the game has seen, but he turned his back on it.

Almost nine years to the day before Studd's career ended at The Oval, he had attended a revivalist meeting close to Eton College with his father and three brothers. The preacher was the American evangelist Dwight L. Moody, who was accompanied by the singer Ira D. Sankey. Studd, guided by his father and by the evangelists, was to dedicate the rest of his life to spreading the Gospel.

In February 1885 he sailed to China, where he was to be a missionary for ten years until driven home by ill health. While there, he had given to charity the fortune that he had inherited from his father on his 25th birthday. Studd believed in the fundamental truths of Christ's teaching, and for him there were no half measures.

From 1895 to 1900 Studd engaged in missionary work in England and

America, and in 1900 he worked with the Anglo-Indian Evangelisation Society. He learned of the state of the multitudes in the Belgian Congo which, at the time, had not been touched by any missionary work, and, in 1913, he set out for that part of Africa which was indeed dark and uncivilised more than half a century ago. He endured dangers, numerous illnesses and many hardships, but he devoted the rest of his life to missionary work in the Congo, and it is there that he died on 16 July 1931.

It should not be imagined that Studd was a 'born cricketer', nor was the game for him just an idle pastime. He dedicated himself to reaching the pinnacle of achievement in the sport, and he treated cricket very seriously. He never regretted that he played cricket, although he later said that he regretted having allowed it to become an idol. He said that by applying himself to the game, he had learned lessons of courage, self-denial and endurance which, in his later work, he was to use to other advantage.

The brevity of his career must deny C.T. Studd a place among the great all-rounders, but the path he chose instead of cricket must surely place him among the best of men.

If Studd were not to take on the mantle of Grace, who then was to become the great all-rounder in succession to the Champion? Grace was, in fact, to reassert himself with his last two 'doubles' in 1885 and 1886, but Flowers, who had accomplished the feat in 1883, was never to repeat it.

Wilfred Flowers was an honest professional who made his mark by twice dismissing Grace when playing for the Colts of England against M.C.C. in 1877. The same year he won a place in the Notts eleven, and he went on to play for the county for twenty seasons. He was an off-break bowler and a resolute batsman. That resolution was seen when he was a member of the M.C.C. side that was beaten in a day by the Australians on 27 May 1878. The Club was out for 19 in its second innings, and Flowers scored 11 of those runs. He made two trips to Australia with Arthur Shrewsbury's sides, but he was selected only once for England in England and that was against Australia at Lord's in 1893.

His life was not attended by the best of luck. His benefits were ruined by bad weather, and failing eyesight forced him to retire from umpiring which he had taken up at the end of his playing career in 1896. He was in every respect a model for the hard-working county all-rounder who was to play such an important part in first-class cricket between the wars. He was loyal and respected but, like William Brockwell of Surrey who did the 'double' in 1899, he was essentially a county cricketer rather than an all-rounder of the very highest level.

Brockwell was a stylish right-handed opening batsman and fast medium pace bowler. He played for England against Australia at Old Trafford in 1893 and went with Stoddart's team to Australia in 1894–95, but he met with little success. His 105 wickets in 1899 were the pinnacle of his achievement with the ball, but he could never be described as Test quality as a bowler. His life ended sadly, for he fell upon hard times once he left first-class cricket.

If Brockwell never fulfilled himself as a top-class all-rounder, George Davidson was never given the opportunity. Arguably, he was the best all-round cricketer that Derbyshire has ever produced. He made his debut for the county in 1886 at the age of 20, and his talent as a stylish right-handed batsman and fast medium pace bowler was immediately recognisable. Derbyshire was one of the weaker counties of the period, and it was hardly likely that Davidson would win international recognition, however manfully he performed.

'Had he been associated with a stronger county, it is likely that he would have enjoyed a still more brilliant career, the fact of being so often on the beaten side having naturally a somewhat depressing effect on his cricket.'

In 1895 he scored 1,296 runs and took 138 wickets, so becoming only the fourth Englishman to achieve the 'double', but there was to be no Test call for Davidson. The following season he hit 274 against Lancashire at Old Trafford, and this remains the highest score ever made for Derbyshire. His main task, however, was to carry the county bowling, and this he did most nobly. His pace increased, and his control remained unerringly accurate. He was strong in constitution, muscle and endeavour, although of medium height.

In 1888 Derbyshire had been demoted to second-class status because of poor results, and did not return to the first rank until 1894. Thus Davidson's first-class appearances were limited to 95 matches, but in these he took 621 wickets and scored 5,546 runs.

In the winter of 1899 Davidson caught influenza and this developed into pneumonia. He died on 8 February. He was 32 years old and at the height of his cricketing prowess. Fate had decreed that he should never receive the highest rewards for his achievements. In this study of the great all-rounders he receives only a passing mention, yet he marked the end of a period which had begun with Grace and suggested the beginning of another which was to feature Hirst, Rhodes, Gunn, Relf, Jackson, Jessop and many others.

For the time being, however, we must turn our attention to Australia and to the first man seriously to challenge Grace's claim to be known as the greatest all-rounder in the world.

3

THE W.G. GRACE OF AUSTRALIA

England prided herself on being the mother of cricket and until the second half of the nineteenth century looked with a somewhat patronising view upon cricket and cricketers from outside her shores. Harry Altham wrote in his *History of Cricket:* 'In the early summer of 1878 so little was understood about Australian cricket that the President of the Cambridge University Cricket Club could actually be mistaken as to the complexions of the gentlemen then about to engage upon their first tour in the Mother Country.'

The Australians were well beaten by a strong Nottinghamshire side in their opening match, but five days later they beat a strong M.C.C. side at Lord's in a day (a match we have noted earlier) and from that moment the fierce and friendly rivalry between the two nations began.

An English team had visited Australia as early as 1862, and the first Test match had been played at Melbourne in March 1877, but 1878 saw the first official visit of an Australian side to England, and that after much opposition. Two years later that opposition had been overcome, and Murdoch brought over the second Australian side. Murdoch was captain again in 1882 and he led what many considered to be the best side to visit England before the First World War. Included in the Australian party of thirteen (Beal, the manager, played in one game) was George Giffen, later to be known as the 'W.G. Grace of Australia'.

George Giffen was born in Adelaide on 27 March 1859. He began his career with the Norwood Club, but later played for West Adelaide. He first represented South Australia in 1880, and for years he virtually was the South Australian team, the outcome of matches depending on his performances.

Broad shouldered, heavily moustached, tall, slim and very strong, Giffen had massive hands which enabled him to turn his off-breaks and aided his off-cutters which were delivered at slow medium pace. He had a 'most puzzling action and a long run'. He flighted the ball cleverly and varied his pace, so that one of his most effective deliveries was the ball he held back – one which he tossed high, but which pitched just short of a length and produced a crop of wickets for him, caught and bowled.

As a batsman, he began as a hitter, but developed the soundest of defences. He possessed a rather crouched stance, but quickly uncoiled to play a wide variety of shots, particularly hard-hit, flowing drives. He fielded well in any position and, like the greatest of all-rounders, he was, and wanted to be, always in the game.

Giffen first played for Australia against England at Melbourne at the turn of the year 1881–82, a few months before his first tour of England, and he shared a fifth wicket partnership of 107 with Tom Horan, Australia's first century partnership in Test cricket. However, his talents were not fully used in that series, nor were they really needed on his first tour of England.

The only Test match of 1882 was the one in which Studd finished with 0 not out, Spofforth took 14 wickets and Australia won by 7 runs. Giffen scored 2 and 0, and his bowling was not needed. Indeed, with Spofforth, Boyle, Garrett and Palmer in the side, Giffen had very limited opportunities for displaying his bowling skill on that first tour. He had his moments of triumph, however, and he played a decisive part in the memorable victory over a very strong Gentlemen of England side at The Oval. He hit 43 and then took 8 for 49 and 3 for 60 as the Australians triumphed by an innings.

He said later that on his first tour of England he had learned much. He learned how to adapt himself to all wickets and all occasions, and how to adhere to basic principles of line and length in bowling and playing straight in batting. He always remained a thinker and, like all great players, a learner.

In 1882 Giffen scored 873 runs, average 18·18, a much better average on the wickets of the period than it would be on the placid tracks of today, and took 32 wickets. That he had few chances with the ball can be seen from the fact Spofforth, Boyle, Palmer and Garrett all took more than 125 wickets each and totalled 598 wickets between them.

Two years later, with Murdoch again captain, Giffen was to play a more prominent part in the side. Before leaving Australia the team assembled in Melbourne and Sydney to play matches against a Combined Team, a side composed of players who had just failed to make the trip, Walter Giffen, George's younger brother, being among them. The first match in Melbourne was drawn. Murdoch scored 279, McDonnel 111 and Giffen 53. He also took 4 for 40. In the return match in Sydney, on 15,

16 and 18 February 1884, the Fourth Australian Team reached 318 on the first day. By the end of the second day the Combined Team had been bowled out for 222 and reduced to 52 for 4 in their second innings. Giffen had taken 3 for 62 in the first innings, and on the final morning completed the most outstanding bowling performance in the history of Australian cricket, taking 10 for 66 as the Combined Team were bowled out for 113. The Fourth Australian Team won by 9 wickets, Giffen being the man out, bowled by Spofforth for 2.

George Giffen's feat of taking all 10 wickets had never before been accomplished outside England, and only three bowlers, Wall, Allen and Brayshaw, have emulated the achievement in Australia in the one hundred and two years since Giffen. Grace twice took all 10 wickets in an innings, once before and once after Giffen's performance.

It was apparent that more bowling would fall on the shoulders of Giffen on his second trip to England, for Garrett was missing and Boyle was past his best. Nine of the thirteen players who had toured in 1882 returned, although the team was handicapped by an injury to Cooper, one of the newcomers, who broke a finger on the voyage to England and was unfit for most of the tour.

The Australians began well enough with an innings victory over Lord Sheffield's XI at Sheffield Park. Giffen and Palmer bowled unchanged throughout both innings, with Giffen taking 10 for 121. There was also a victory over Surrey, but the performance of the side was inconsistent and they were badly beaten by M.C.C. and by the Gentlemen of England as they struggled to find their form. At Old Trafford, Giffen took 6 for 55 and performed the hat trick when he dismissed Taylor, Robinson and D.Q. Steel. He followed this by hitting 113, with 11 fours, in Australia's second innings before rain ended the match.

The run-up to the Test matches continued to show the Australians in uncertain form, and this uncertainty continued through the three-Test series. It was the first time in England that three Test matches had been scheduled for the summer. England won one, and the other two were drawn, with Australia having the better of both. The last match of the season saw the Smokers play the Non-Smokers at Lord's. Giffen appeared for the Smokers, as did Spofforth and Palmer, but the Non-Smokers were the winners. Giffen completed a thousand runs for the tour and took 82 wickets. He was 25 years old and emerging as an all-rounder of outstanding ability.

When Giffen returned to England with the fifth Australian side of 1886 his all-round potential was fully realised. He became the first cricketer

George Giffen. His passion for the game did not diminish with age. He was the first of the great Australian all-rounders.

after Grace, Studd and Flowers to perform the 'double', scoring 1,453 runs and taking 159 wickets. He topped both the batting and the bowling averages, and was the only success of an unhappy tour. At one stage he took 40 wickets in five successive innings.

It had been generally expected that Giffen would captain the fifth Australian side of 1886, but the tour was made under the auspices of the Melbourne Cricket Club and H.J.H. Scott was named as captain. Scott did not have the sense of authority necessary to deal with the disagreements that broke out among the players, and a great deal of friction developed before a match was even played. These quarrels affected the performance of the side, and the bowlers, Giffen, Garrett and Spofforth apart, took a terrible hammering from the England batsmen.

It is doubtful whether Giffen would have made much difference had he been captain. For all his qualities as one of the greatest all-rounders in the history of the game, he was not a good captain. He was to lead Australia on four occasions in 1894-95, but it was said of him that he never knew when to take himself off and that his idea of a change of bowling simply meant that he bowled from the other end.

For the next few years Giffen was content to perform great deeds in his own country. He took 8 for 83 and 4 for 104 for South Australia against Victoria in February 1887, and still finished on the losing side. Later the same year two England teams toured Australia, Mr G.F. Vernon's side, led by Lord Hawke, and Arthur Shrewsbury's team, with C. Aubrey Smith as captain. Vernon's side began their tour with a match against South Australia at Adelaide.

The game was an eventful one for Giffen. He took 5 for 32 in the English side's first innings, finishing with the hat trick, and then, in the state side's second innings, he ran out three of his own partners. The last of the three was his brother Walter, and there was an altercation with the umpire as to which batsman was out. After a delay it was George who continued his innings, and he went on to make 81.

In the return match, played over the Christmas period, he took 5 for 163, but saw South Australia bowled out for 143 and follow-on 239 runs behind. Giffen batted at number three in the second innings, shared a second wicket partnership of 192 with Godfrey, and batted 530 minutes to reach 203 which included 14 fours.

A few weeks later he hit 166 and took 8 for 65 and 6 for 60 as South Australia beat Victoria by an innings, but he did not play for Australia during the season and declined the invitation to tour England with McDonnell's side. He again refused to tour in 1890 when Murdoch took a largely inexperienced side to England, and he earned the reputation of selecting which tours and big matches suited him, often refusing to play unless his brother Walter, a far inferior cricketer, was also chosen.

Whatever the reasons for Giffen's reluctance to tour and his apparent aloofness, none could deny that he had now succeeded Grace as the world's greatest all-rounder. He began the 1891–92 Australian season with what H.S. Altham has rightly described as 'the greatest all-round performance in all recorded cricket of any class'. Batting at number three for South Australia against Victoria at Adelaide, he batted for seven hours to score 271 and then took 9 for 96 as the visitors were put out for 235. When Victoria followed-on he took 7 for 70, and South Australia won by an innings.

In his first encounter with Lord Sheffield's team in 1891–92 Giffen took 7 for 152, and he played a vital part in Australia's victory in the second Test match of the series which gave them the rubber. The game was at Sydney and, in spite of Giffen taking 4 for 88, Australia trailed by 162 on the first innings. Some dour batting took them to 391 in their second innings, so that England were asked to make 230 to win. Giffen took 6 for 72, and Australia won a memorable victory by 72 runs.

Giffen accepted the invitation to tour England in 1893, but the Australian side struggled for want of a fast bowler and lost the one Test that was decided. Giffen, with 142 wickets and 1,220 runs, again did the 'double'. He completed a remarkable 'treble' on his fifth and last tour in 1896, when he scored 1,208 runs and captured 117 wickets. At the time only W.G. Grace had a comparable record.

In 1896 Giffen took his second hat trick in England in the match against an England XI at Wembley, and three years earlier he had played innings of 180 against Gloucestershire and 171 against Yorkshire. His final Test match appearances came in the 1896 series. He scored 80 in the second Test, which Australia won thrillingly by 3 wickets to level the series, but in the last Test he was out for 0 and 1. He dismissed Grace and Ranjitsinhji in England's first innings.

Giffen hit only one Test hundred and that was when he scored 161 against England at Sydney in December 1894. He made 41 in the second innings and had match figures of 8 for 239, thus becoming the only person to score 200 runs and take 8 wickets in an England-Australia Test match. Before we criticise the fact that he only once reached a hundred in a Test match, we should remember that Grace and Ranjitsinhji hit only two apiece. Runs were harder to come by and Tests were fewer in the nineteenth century than they are today.

It is amusing to note that when Giffen performed his great all-round feat at Sydney in 1894 he still finished on the losing side. He maintained his form with 269 runs and 26 wickets in the remaining four Tests, but Australia, under his captaincy, lost 3–2. His 34 wickets in the series remained a record for Australia until beaten by Arthur Mailey in 1920–21.

Giffen continued to play for South Australia until 1903–04 when he was 45 years old. He trained specially for the game against Victoria at Adelaide in 1902–03, for he was within a couple of weeks of his 44th birthday. His effort was rewarded as he scored 81 and 97 not out and had match figures of 15 for 185.

His passion for cricket never diminished. In 1898 his book *With Bat and Ball* was published and it remains an invaluable work for students of the game of the Victorian era. Like the man, the book is warm-hearted, direct and shows a deep reverence for the game itself.

In 1922–23 the match between South Australia and Victoria at Adelaide was played for Giffen's benefit, and in 1925 he retired from his work as a letter sorter in the General Post Office. He had worked there for forty-three years, and it is generally believed that his work helped him to develop the spinning fingers of his massive hands.

In his later life Giffen gave much time and care to the coaching of teams of boys. They began play in the Adelaide Park Lands punctually at 6.00 a.m., and Giffen would remain with them for over two hours. He also took the boys' international and inter-state matches and made running comments on the play. His comments were so illuminating and perceptive that at big matches a regular circle would form round him to enjoy what he had to say and to learn from it. Giffen died on 29 November 1927, and he was greatly mourned.

The years have not lessened Giffen's reputation. He was the W.G. Grace of Australia, the founder of a dynasty of great all-rounders. He was the first of seven Australians who have taken a hundred wickets and scored a thousand runs in Test cricket, and of those that followed him, only Benaud, Miller and Noble can be classed as true all-rounders. Although they scored valuable runs and, in the case of Lindwall, hit two Test centuries, neither Davidson nor Lindwall could lay claim to a place in a side on their ability as batsmen, while Ian Johnson did not reach the highest level as either batsman or bowler.

Giffen was honoured by having a grandstand named after him at Adelaide Oval, and his immediate successor in the Australian side, Monty Noble, was honoured in the same way at the Sydney Cricket Ground.

There are many who would place Noble above Giffen as Australia's greatest all-rounder. Certainly, there is no one in the history of the game whose life was more devoted to sportsmanship and all that is good and true in cricket. In one aspect of the game, captaincy, he was far superior to Giffen, and it is doubtful if Australia could have had a better leader.

Montague Alfred Noble was born in Sydney in 1873. He thrived in junior cricket and was taken to New Zealand with a New South Wales side in 1893. The following season he hit 152 not out for Eighteen Sydney Juniors against A.E. Stoddart's team. This innings won him a place in the state side and he quickly established himself as an all-rounder of outstanding merit.

Noble was more than 6 feet tall and weighed 13 stone. He was quick and agile in the field and was outstanding at cover point in his generation. As a batsman he played whatever game was necessary for his side. He was upright and elegant, beautifully relaxed and positioned, able to hit very hard and able to defend relentlessly and uncompromisingly. He used his height to great advantage when hitting the ball, for he had the full range of strokes.

His bowling was unique. He was an off-spinner who could vary his pace from slow to medium fast off his fairly long run. He had immaculate control and possessed the ability to swerve the ball. This ability came from his grip which he had learned from American baseball players who had toured Australia. He had lean, bony fingers and, holding the ball between thumb and forefinger, he could impart 'curve' or swing. After the ball pitched, it spun or swung late, and Noble was devastating on a damp wicket. His success as a bowler when he first entered Test cricket had as much to do with the element of surprise he evoked as with his innate ability.

Noble was chosen to play for Australia in the second Test match at Melbourne in January 1898. Hugh Trumble, a great all-rounder, but one who was more renowned for his bowling, was in the Australian side and he was to influence Noble quite strongly. Noble was captivated by Trumble's eager run to the wicket and his variation in pace. Australia made 520, and England, with Trumble taking four wickets and Noble taking the wicket of Wainwright, were bowled out for 315. In the second innings Noble took over and captured 6 for 49, as Australia won by an innings and 55 runs. Australia won the next Test by an innings, and Noble had match figures of 8 for 162. Fifteen wickets in his first two Test matches were a remarkable beginning for the young all-rounder.

Hugh Trumble and Noble were both in the side that came to England in 1899, and Trumble completed the 'double'. Noble showed superb all-round form and stamped his name indelibly on the history of Test cricket with his deeds at Old Trafford. He hit a century on his first appearance in England, 116 not out against South of England at Crystal Palace, and showed his qualities as a thinking cricketer by realising the need to adapt both his batting and bowling technique to English conditions when it was necessary.

The first Test was drawn, but Australia won the second match at Lord's, with Victor Trumper scoring his first Test hundred and Noble making 54, sharing a stand of 130 with Clem Hill who also hit a hundred. The third Test was drawn when rain ended play with England likely winners.

For the first time, five Tests were to be played in a series in England, and the teams gathered at Old Trafford for the fourth encounter. Noble sent back Quaife and MacLaren, and England were 47 for 4, but Tom Hayward hit 130 so that the home side recovered to 372. Australia were soon in trouble. They were 14 for 3 when Noble went to the wicket, and soon they were 57 for 7.

Noble had gone to the wicket at 11.25 a.m., and when Australia were all out for 196 at 3.30 p.m. was 60 not out. Under the existing laws the follow-on was automatically applied when a side trailed by 120 runs or more, and it was the events of this match which caused the law to be changed.

Australia began their second innings with Noble and Worrall as the opening pair. They put on 93 before Worrall was out. At the close of play Noble was 59 not out. He was the first man in the history of Test cricket to have scored two fifties in a day. His innings continued into the last day. At one period he went 45 minutes without scoring a run as he concentrated all his mind and all his energy on saving the game for Australia.

At 2.45 p.m. on the last afternoon Noble gave J.T. Hearne a return catch. He had made 89. His two innings had occupied 510 minutes, and he had performed one of the greatest rescue acts in the history of cricket. He was not by nature a stonewaller, but the needs of the side had dictated the way that he should bat. He was a thinker, a tactician with a total knowledge of the game. In contrast, he hit four centuries in succession for New South Wales between 1898 and 1900, and on his second tour to England in 1902 he scored 284 against Sussex at Hove, he and Warwick Armstrong putting on 428 for the sixth wicket.

The 1902 side was again led by Joe Darling, and Noble 'by now a superb player, took the all-round honours in a team of stars'. He scored

1,416 runs and took 98 wickets, but Warwick Armstrong, on his first tour, was only a little behind him.

Noble had been in devastating form when MacLaren had brought the England side to Australia in the previous winter. England had won the first Test, but on the first day of the second Test 25 wickets fell on a rain-affected pitch. England were all out for 61 in 68 minutes. Noble was unplayable and took 7 for 17. At the time, only Albert Trott had recorded a better performance for Australia against England. Australia made 353 in their second innings, and when England went in again Noble took 6 for 60, his six victims coming in the first seven, and Australia levelled the series. Australia won the last three Tests and Noble finished the series with 32 wickets at 19·00 runs each. Only Giffen had bettered this and, in a five-match series, only Mailey and Lawson have beaten it since.

The first two Tests of the 1902 series were marred by rain and were drawn, but Noble took 11 for 103 at Bramall Lane, Sheffield, and Australia won. They clinched the series with a three-run win at Old Trafford.

So desperate had England's plight become by the time that Joe Darling led the 1905 side to England, that M.C.C. had taken over responsibility for the selection of the England side. They did this in 1903–04 when Warner took the England side to Australia. Noble captained Australia for the first time and hit 133 at Sydney in his first match as captain, but Warner's men won the series in spite of his efforts, and England held on to the 'Ashes' against Darling's team in 1905.

Noble hit six centuries on the tour, scored 2,084 runs and took 59 wickets, but little went right in the Tests. Warwick Armstrong did the 'double', and he was to equal Giffen's record of three 'doubles' on his tours to England.

Armstrong upset critics on the 1905 tour by bowling leg-theory to a packed on-side field for hours on end, and this was not to be the last time that he irked followers of the game in England, but he took 87 wickets and scored 2,863 runs in Test cricket and was unbeaten as captain of Australia in ten Tests. Noted for his clashes with authority, Armstrong was a big man. He stood 6 feet, 2 inches, and at the end of his career weighed 22 stone. He still managed to bowl his leg-breaks and top-spinners to great effect, and was a tremendous hitter of the ball. The character has tended to obscure the quality of the cricketer, for all the legends that surround Armstrong concern his whisky-drinking and his perversity. Nevertheless, he was respected by other players and in 1905 he hit 1,902 runs and took 122 wickets, a show of all-round strength which few others have approached. He was not, however, in the same class as Giffen, Noble, Benaud, and Miller.

Noble was entrusted with the captaincy again when A.O. Jones took England to Australia in 1907–08. Australia won the series by four Tests to one, and Noble was hailed as one of the very great captains as well as one of the very great all-rounders.

He led the thirteenth Australian side to England in 1909 and, although his powers as an all-rounder had somewhat diminished, he took 25 wickets and scored 1,109 runs on the tour. His stature as a cricketer now stood higher than ever. He proved himself 'a courageous and enterprising commander by his control of the side'.

The Australians began disastrously, losing three matches, including the first Test by 10 wickets, inside the first month. 'Then came a great example of bold, shrewd tactics. Winning the toss at Lord's, Noble gave England first innings under favourable batting conditions, and his enterprising venture upset a badly chosen eleven. The England batting was poor, catches were dropped, and Noble practically settled the issue by bowling A.C. MacLaren, his rival captain, with an astonishing break-back in the second innings. Australia won by nine wickets, and from that point all went well.'

The break-back which bowled MacLaren was, in fact, Noble's last wicket in Test cricket. He bowled only a few overs in the remainder of the series (which was won by Australia), and he ended his international career at The Oval with an innings of 55. He played for New South Wales until shortly after the First World War.

Noble's all-round strength was based on his unwavering belief in his own ability and the intelligence to provide whatever was needed to win or to save a match. He believed in team cricket, and he shaped his performance to the requirements of the side. He knew the strengths and weaknesses of all his opponents, and his field placings in frustrating the favourite strokes of batsmen were revolutionary in their day. Above all, he was capable of getting the best from those under him, demanding only that they gave all to the game and took it as seriously as he did.

Having been a bank clerk and a dentist, he turned to writing and broadcasting when he left the game, and he remained one of the most respected of all men.

When Noble died in 1940, *Wisden* suggested that his figures proved that there had been no superior all-rounder in Test cricket. At the time only Giffen, Rhodes and Noble had achieved the 'double' in Test cricket, and Noble played in fewer Tests than the others. Indeed, Noble reached the mark in 27 Tests, and although this has since been bettered by Mankad, Kapil Dev and Botham, arguably they had some 'softer' opposition than Noble encountered in the Golden Age.

Giffen was dubbed the 'W.G. Grace of Australia', and commentators as diverse as Clem Hill, the Australian captain, and Harry Altham, the cricket historian, have argued that he was the greatest of Australian all-rounders. Noble's challenge is indeed a strong one. He was not only a great all-rounder in all three departments of the game, but was also a very great captain. One thing is certain: he followed a standard of manners, behaviour, commitment and application which, were it followed by some who play today, would make cricket a better game.

4

THE YORKSHIRE CONNECTION

The final years of the nineteenth century saw the recognition of the all-rounder as an essential member of any successful side. In 1894 *Wisden*, having honoured batsmen and bowlers, felt that attention should be drawn to the all-rounders of outstanding quality who were now gracing the game and named Giffen, Alec Hearne, G.H.S. Trott, Wainwright and F.S. Jackson as its five cricketers of the year.

Harry Trott was an elegant, forcing right-hand bat and leg-spin bowler, who had toured England with the Australian side in 1893 and was to return as captain in 1896. Alec Hearne was also a right-hand bat, who bowled his leg-breaks at a quicker pace than Trott and did noble work for Kent. He played only once for England and that was against South Africa in Cape Town in 1892. Ted Wainwright was one of the mainstays of Lord Hawke's great Yorkshire side. He was a right-handed batsman and an off-break bowler who was particularly effective on a wearing wicket. He was to do the 'double' in 1897, but in his five Test matches, played when he was with A.E. Stoddart's team in Australia the following winter, he scored only 132 runs and failed to take a wicket. The fifth member of *Wisden*'s group, F.S. Jackson, was also a Yorkshireman.

Colonel The Honourable Sir Francis Stanley Jackson, PC, GCIE, was one of those talents of whom we lesser mortals despair. He seemed to be able to do everything. Born near Leeds, the son of a Cabinet Minister, he flourished at Harrow, where Winston Churchill was his fag, and at Cambridge. He led Cambridge to victory over Oxford in 1893 and showed such fine form with bat and ball that he was invited to play for England against Australia at Lord's. He scored 91, but bowled only five overs. In the next Test, at The Oval, he hit 103.

His own account of the events at The Oval is amusing. W.G. Grace said to him: 'With all these batsmen I don't know where to put you.' 'Anywhere will do.' 'Then number seven.' 'Thanks. That's my lucky number; I was the seventh child.' 'And that match brought me my first hundred for Engand. Mold came in last when I was 99. He nearly ran me out, so in desperation I jumped in and drove Giffen high to the seats, reaching 103. Then the bewildered Mold did run me out.' In 1893 a hit into the seats was worth only four runs and not the six with which a batsman would be credited today.

Jackson was unable to make any trips to Australia because of his business commitments, and when the third Test match against Australia was played at Old Trafford on 24, 25 and 26 August 1893, he chose instead to play for Yorkshire against Sussex at Hove. He played in all the Test matches of 1896 and 1899, but although he thrived as a batsman, his bowling was used sparingly. This pattern was repeated in the series of 1902, when he was England's leading batsman with fifties at Edgbaston and Lord's and a magnificent 128 at Old Trafford.

England were 44 for 5, but he and Len Braund, an aggressive right-handed batsman and leg-break bowler and, according to C.B. Fry, one of the greatest of all-rounders, added 141. Jackson played a great innings. However, that evening at dinner a distinguished lady turned to him and said: 'I was so disappointed that Ranjitsinhji failed', making no mention of his own marvellous effort.

His greatest year, however, was 1905, his final year of Test cricket. He was captain of England, and no England skipper has ever given a finer all-round display. He topped the England batting averages with 492 runs, average 70·28, and headed the bowling averages with 13 wickets, average 15·46. He hit two centuries, won the toss five times out of five, and England won the series two–nil and had the better of the three drawn matches.

England were bowled out for 196, Jackson 0, in the first innings of the first Test, and Australia, 129 for 1, were looking set for a big lead before Jackson took the wickets of Noble, Hill and Darling in one over. He finished with 5 for 52. In the second innings he scored 82 not out, shared an unbeaten stand of 113 with Wilfred Rhodes, and England went on to win by 213 runs. In the fourth Test, at Old Trafford, he hit his second hundred in successive Tests and became the only batsman to score five hundreds against Australia in England.

He first played for Yorkshire in 1890 and he last appeared for them in 1907. For Yorkshire against Lancashire in 1902 he took 8 for 13 and, the same year, he and George Hirst bowled out the Australians for 23 at Leeds. Jackson took the final 4 wickets in five balls and finished with 5 for 12. His one and only 'double' came in 1899, and it was that year that Lyttleton wrote of him: 'At the present, indeed, he stands in quite the first

The Hon. F. S. Jackson. A man of many talents, he had judgement, determination, exceptional courage and an unswerving belief in his own abilities.

rank of cricketers, whether English or Colonials, and I am inclined to think that, if I had to choose a side, my first choice would be Jackson.'

He was a strong, well-built man of nearly 6 feet in height and, according to C.B. Fry, was 'exceptionally good-looking in the Anglo-Saxon Guards officer way'. He was impeccable in dress and walked briskly on to the field as if eager to do battle with the enemy. To his physical strength he added qualities of calm, authoritative judgement, determination and 'above all, exceptional courage which amounted to belief in his own abilities.' The quality of belief in oneself is one which is shared by all the greatest all-rounders from Grace to Noble, from Procter to Botham.

As a batsman he was stylish and free, a forward player, strong in the drive. Fry, not the easiest of critics, was fulsome in his praise:

'Not only has he an extraordinary number of different strokes of all kinds, but he has a quite notable ability of adapting these strokes without altering them, except in the matter of timing, to all kinds of bowling and to all kinds of wickets. Many batsmen, and good ones, have one game for fast wickets and another for slow, one for good-length bowling and another for bad-length bowling. F.S. Jackson has one game of a most comprehensive and elastic kind which he plays with consummate confidence always, and which he brings into effective relation with all conditions of play. Perhaps, among modern batsmen, there is no one who maintains what may be described as perpetual uniformity of style on every kind of wicket and against every kind of bowling as he does, with the possible exception of Victor Trumper.

'Probably the secret of this uniformity is nothing more nor less than a settled habit of watching the ball from the bowler's hand to the pitch, and from the pitch on to the bat, and of taking every ball as it comes absolutely and entirely on its independent merits; and then – of just playing it quite naturally. Such a method brings the easy and the difficult into the same plane, provided the batsman has versatility and what, for want of a better name, we call genius.'

Perhaps an even greater compliment was paid by his first adversary, George Giffen, who saw Jackson only in his early days: 'He is certainly one of the finest and at the same time most judicious forcing batsmen England has produced in many a day . . . On true Australian wickets he would prove a tough nut to crack.'

He bowled right-arm fast medium with an easy, rhythmic action and he moved the ball prodigiously, particularly in from the off. Lord Hawke, whose presence in the Yorkshire side denied Jackson the captaincy of the county except on rare occasions, placed Jackson in the very highest class as a bowler. Writing in *Wisden* 1932, Hawke said: 'I have never seen Jacker's equal at bowling for his field. I remember one occasion when we were "in the cart" at Bradford against Surrey how precisely he bowled for his field, and how he apologised to me for having bowled a ball not intended. Though his grand batting for England is best remembered, he was a bowler of the very highest class, with a graceful, flowing delivery of a kind but rarely seen nowadays.'

Lord Hawke's emphasis is an important one; so often do we dwell on the batting of Grace, Sobers or Miller that we forget their might as bowlers.

Jackson played only twice in 1906 and once in 1907, and after that he concentrated on other matters. When he gave up cricket he took up golf, and it is said that he spent the whole of one winter practising strokes in front of the mirror, referring to textbooks, but never striking a ball on the course. When he finally got on to the golf-course he was very quickly playing off a handicap of one. Such relentless pursuit of perfection was typical of the man.

In the Boer War Jackson served with the Royal Lancaster Regiment of Militia, and in the First World War he was Lieutenant-Colonel of a West Yorkshire Regiment which he raised and commanded. He was Unionist MP for the Howdenshire Division of Yorkshire from 1915 to 1926, first Financial Secretary to the War Office and then Chairman of the Unionist Party Organisation. In 1927 he became Governor of Bengal and survived an assassination attempt. He was President of M.C.C. in 1921 and Chairman of Selectors in 1934. He was bombed out in 1940, run over by a taxi in 1946 and died in 1947 in his 77th year. His memorial service was conducted by Canon F.H. Gillingham, the former Essex cricketer, who described Jackson as the most honest man he had ever met: 'I never heard him say an unkind word about anyone, and he always had excuses for anyone who spoke an unkind word to him.'

In his charming book, *Jackson's Year*, Alan Gibson suggested that it was 'no exaggeration to say that he was one of the very best cricketers – perhaps *the* best all-rounder, saving W.G. Grace – ever to represent England, as well as being a great gentleman.' Supporters of Botham may well argue with Alan Gibson, as may Yorkshiremen who might well forward two others of their number who played alongside Jackson.

When *Wisden* selected their five all-rounders of the year in 1894 they did not choose George Herbert Hirst, for although he had taken 99 wickets and finished fourth in the national averages in 1893, he had scored only

376 runs and was considered primarily a bowler. He had been an integral part of Yorkshire's triumph in the county championship, but he was only 21 years old.

The magazine *Cricket* had singled him out as 'A Coming Bowler', and in August 1893 he related his tale to them as their feature player. He had begun to play for his village club, Kirkheaton, at the age of 14, but it was not until 1889 that he became known outside his club.

'In that year Kirkheaton won the Huddersfield Cricket Cup, and as I had done my share in the matches, I was asked to play for somebody who couldn't turn up in the match, Yorkshire against Cheshire, on this very ground (Huddersfield) in that year.'

He did not do too well:

'I scored an innings of 6 runs, and I didn't bowl a ball. I suppose I was, as you say, a bit nervous, not funky exactly, but I was so well known on this ground, and a few friends turned up specially to see how I should shape, that it was not to be wondered at I did next to nothing. Next year I got another chance, against Essex this time, but with no better results; I had two innings, one not out, but made no runs, whilst in bowling I took no wicket for the 17 runs they scored off me. The year after I was not tried at all for the County, and I didn't know if they would want me again.'

He left Kirkheaton for Elland, then Mirfield, before going to Huddersfield who engaged him from 1892 onwards. He considered that his experiences with Huddersfield shaped his future. He learned to adapt his bowling to wickets and to batsmen, and he improved so rapidly that he was put into the Yorkshire side in 1892 and played regularly in 1893. He was also a considerable rugby player, performing at centre three-quarter for Mirfield and displaying a good pair of hands.

He batted right and he bowled left, and he modelled himself on nobody. Initially, he used to bowl as fast as he could: 'I always bowl fast, never put in a slow one, taking care not to bowl beyond my strength. The fact is, any slows I might send down would be sure to be knocked all over the place.'

He was enthusiastic and justly proud of his youthful achievements. He was an extrovert who played cricket with gusto and optimism. He never gave up hope until the last wicket had fallen, always believing that victory could be achieved or a match saved against the greatest of odds. He found joy wherever he went.

His achievements in 1894 were almost identical to those of the previous season, and Lord Hawke said of him: 'He is a young bowler, fastish left-arm, with a nice action, straight and quick. He is a number ten batsman.'

George Hirst. Sir Home Gordon said of him 'If I had to have one man to play for me to save my life . . . it would have been George Hirst.'

The dismissal of his batting was somewhat harsh, for although he scored only 564 runs in 1894, he did hit his first first-class hundred, 115 not out against Gloucestershire.

The following season he took 150 wickets and scored 710 runs, and in 1896 he performed the 'double' for the first time. In all, he was to accomplish the feat fourteen times, and only one other man (Rhodes) has ever bettered that and ever will.

He was essentially a self-taught batsman, quick of foot and eye. As befits one who began as a tail-ender with a desire to bowl as quickly as possible, George Hirst wanted to hit hard and often. He hooked and pulled viciously, and only in Australia, which he toured twice with moderate results, was his liking for the hook ever a liability. The batsman whom Lord Hawke had decreed was a natural number ten scored a thousand runs in a season nineteen times, and in 1905 he hit 341 against Leicestershire at Leicester, which remains the highest innings ever scored for Yorkshire even though Sutcliffe, Holmes, Hutton and Boycott were to come. He hit 54 boundaries in that innings, and his ferocious hitting could put a field to rout. An eyewitness recalled an incident at Taunton when he pulled the ball massively and skyed it: 'It looked like going to cover-point, but then swung away in the high wind, and eventually landed behind the square-leg umpire – with half the fielding side giving chase and no one getting anywhere near it.'

In his first match after the First World War, he made 180 not out in five hours for Yorkshire against M.C.C. at Lord's. He was 48 years old. In 1920 he became coach at Eton, but he still played for Yorkshire on occasions until 1929 when, at the age of 58, he played against M.C.C. in the Scarborough Festival. Bill Bowes was opposed to him in that match. The big crowd applauded him all the way to the wicket. George was given a single. His partner, Robinson, scored a single and Hirst was again facing Bill Bowes:

'I swear I tried to present him with more runs and tried to bowl an inswinger pitching on the leg stump and running down the leg side either to be pushed, glanced or swept as George fancied. But, Oh dear; although I did not bowl it as fast as normal, I delivered one of the best outswingers I've ever bowled in my life. The ball pitched on the leg stump but swung back like a fast leg-break and clipped off the off bail.

'George looked his surprise and then walked up the pitch and said: "Bill, young man. When I was good I should have had a job to stop that, now I haven't a chance. Well bowled. It was a beauty." He turned and walked back to the pavilion with the crowd still cheering. He was as popular as ever.'

Hirst had no need to worry at scoring only one in his last innings and failing to take a wicket in the twenty-three overs he bowled in the match. He had scored 36,203 runs and taken 2,727 wickets in his career, and when he caught J.W.H.T. Douglas in the first innings it was his 550th catch. He took most of them at mid-off, where he was considered the best in the game. They were generally off scorching drives at a time when driving was the most prolific of a batsman's scoring strokes.

He first played for England in Sydney, in December 1897, the Test before Noble made his debut for Australia, and he first played against Australia in England at Trent Bridge, in June 1899 (Grace's last Test). His record in Test matches was not as good as one might have expected, but he had some memorable moments. He and Wilfred Rhodes bowled out Australia for 36 in the first Test at Edgbaston in 1902. Hirst took the wickets of Trumper, Hill and S.E. Gregory for 15 runs. The match after this Test was the one in which Jackson and Hirst, 5 for 9, bowled out the Australians for 23.

A.C. MacLaren, the England captain, caused a controversy which still rages today when he left Hirst out of the side for the fourth Test at Old Trafford and played Fred Tate. Tate dropped a vital catch, was bowled for four, and England lost by 3 runs. Poor Tate never played Test cricket again, but Hirst was back for the final game at The Oval. He took 5 for 77 and scored 43, but England trailed by 141 runs on the first innings. Eventually, England had to make 263 to win. Gilbert Jessop hit his only century in Test cricket, which, as it came in 75 minutes, was at the time the fastest in Test history, but when the ninth wicket fell England were still 15 short of victory. Hirst was the not out batsman, and he was joined by his great friend Wilfred Rhodes. Hirst walked to meet Rhodes on his way to the wicket and muttered the words which have become immortal in the Hirst and Yorkshire legend – 'We'll get 'em in singles, Wilfred' – and they did.

If Hirst's success in his twenty-four Tests was limited (790 runs and 59 wickets), he was, in the Golden Age of cricket, described as 'the greatest county cricketer of all time'. Few could argue with that statement for Hirst has the figures to prove it, and his buoyancy, tenacity, ready wit and perpetual good humour made him one of the most loved of cricketers. In the years of the Yorkshire championship hat trick, 1900–02, he took 328 wickets and scored 5,323 runs, yet his greatest years as an all-rounder were 1904–06.

In the first two of these seasons, he emulated W.G. Grace's record of 1876 by scoring two thousand runs and taking a hundred wickets. In 1906 he established a record which, under the existing system of county cricket, will never be beaten. He hit 2,385 runs and took 208 wickets. He produced some remarkable performances that season. At Catford he hit 101 and had match figures of 11 for 79 against Kent, while at Bath he hit 111 and 117 not out and took 6 for 70 and 5 for 45 against Somerset.

The mighty achievement of 1906 brought in its wake several stories which have passed into cricket folklore. Years after the event he was asked if he thought that anyone would ever beat his record. With his usual twinkle he replied, 'I don't know, but whoever does it will be very tired.' His own favourite tale was of the boy at Eton who came to him and said, 'Excuse me, sir, but are you the Mr Hirst who scored two thousand runs and took two hundred wickets in a season?' 'Yes, that's me,' answered Hirst. The boy looked him up and down and then said simply, 'My God.'

No man gave more encouragement to young players or helped them more, and he was revered at Eton and in Yorkshire as a coach. He had fought hard to participate in first-class cricket, and that he never forgot it is shown by a maxim which he took with him through his playing days: 'I will help every young cricketer who comes into the side, but I'll make him fight like the devil to take my place.'

He was fit and he was tough, and he could bowl for hours and bat for as long as he was needed. He wanted to be playing the game all the time.

The power of his bowling did not lie in his speed, but in his 'swerver' which he developed at the beginning of the century. He had a long, bounding run, an easy action and he could make the ball dip into the batsman very late. He discovered that he could best 'swerve' the new ball, and when bowling into the wind. He studied the phenomenon and exaggerated his delivery stride, experimenting with it. He bowled with three specialist fielders at short leg. One of the first to exploit leg theory, he was indeed the father of modern seam and swing bowling, for, before Hirst showed its possibilities, bowlers had rubbed the new ball in the dirt to take off the polish and shine.

In Yorkshire they will not tell you who has been the greatest all-rounder since W.G. Grace. They will only say that he batted right and bowled left and that he came from Kirkheaton.

Hirst strained a leg muscle on the tour of Australia in 1897–98, and he struggled through most of the 1898 season in England missing many matches. This, however, was an important season for Yorkshire cricket. It was the year that Wilfred Rhodes made his debut in first-class cricket.

Yorkshire cricket has always been at its strongest when the county has fielded a slow left-arm bowler of quality. Peate, Peel, Rhodes, Verity, Wardle – it is a distinguished line, and arguably the White Rose county has never flourished since the departure of Johnny Wardle for whom no adequate replacement was ever found.

In 1897 Robert Peel was a very fine bowler and a good batsman, but he was banished from the Yorkshire side by Lord Hawke for conduct unbecoming. His predecessor, Edmund Peate, had suffered a similar fate. So, in 1898 Yorkshire were looking for a slow left-arm bowler. For the opening tour of the season two such bowlers were selected, Rhodes and Cordingley. Wilfred Rhodes played in the first match, against M.C.C. at Lord's, took 6 for 63, and was never again omitted from a Yorkshire side for which he was available. Cordingley played in one non-first-class match, against Worcestershire, and then moved to play a few games for Sussex. Rhodes finished his first season with an astounding 154 wickets. He was to take more than fifty wickets in every season in which he played first-class cricket from 1898 until 1930, and was to exceed one hundred wickets in twenty-three of his twenty-nine seasons in the game.

He was the personification of Yorkshire cricket: shrewd, dour, observant, meticulous, thinking and unostentatious. He was the complement to his friend Hirst, who had forwarded his claims for a place in the Yorkshire side.

At the age of eighteen Rhodes was club professional at Galashiels. He bowled medium pace, but noted that his slower ball was bringing consistent success. He spent a winter practising on his own in a barn, experimenting with spinning a ball on which he had chalked lines. In the spring he bowled against a haystack and mastered flight and length. The folk at Galashiels noted his quality and advised him to seek a first-class cricket career in England. He answered an advertisement by Warwickshire, was accepted on to the ground staff and then rejected because the county had financial difficulties. Hirst brought him to Yorkshire.

His success was the fruit of his labour. He had taught himself much, practised much and followed his ambition with a determination and a resolution that was to mark all his cricket. However, he was blessed with natural gifts; he was born a great bowler. He had a feel for the ball and caressed it and spun it with his strong fingers. On a true pitch, as in Australia, he tantalised with flight and length; on a worn wicket he was unplayable because of his ability to turn the ball sharply. His approach to the wicket was almost a walk, but the turn of the body propelled the ball at a quicker pace than many would have anticipated and the spin was

Hirst and Rhodes. Who, W. G. apart, was the greatest all-rounder? Yorkshiremen will tell you that he batted right-hand and bowled left; and he came from Kirkheaton. Hirst and Rhodes were the great all-rounders of the golden age.

acute. Above all, he bowled with his brain. He deluded batsmen. He waged a psychological war with them which he invariably won, and which brought forth one of his most famous and wise remarks: 'If batsmen thinks as I'm spinnin' them, then I am.'

Although he was born to bowl, he was never incompetent with the bat and, quietly effective, in the spirit of the true all-rounder he always wanted to be in the game. Yorkshire wanted him as a bowler, and Lord Hawke marked him down as a number eleven, just as he had decreed that Hirst was a number ten. Yorkshire had batsmen who could make the runs they needed, and Hawke discouraged Rhodes from staying at the crease too long, suggesting that twenty runs should be his maximum. Rhodes, however, had other ideas. He hit 557 runs in his first season, including 78 against Middlesex, and in 1901 he hit a maiden first-class hundred, for Yorkshire against M.C.C. at Scarborough.

He had only been playing for Yorkshire for a season when he was picked to play for England against Australia at Trent Bridge (W.G.'s last Test). Rhodes batted number ten (he was number eleven in the other Tests in which he played during the series), opened the bowling, took 4 for 58 in the first innings and 3 for 60 in the second.

In 1902 he and George Hirst bowled out Australia for 36. Rhodes had 7 for 17. England lost the series, and Rhodes, 4 not out, was left high and dry when Fred Tate was bowled at Old Trafford to give Australia victory by 3 runs. He and Hirst gained some revenge at The Oval.

The revenge became total when Pelham Warner took the M.C.C. team to Australia in 1903–04. In the first Test, at Sydney, Rhodes took 2 for 41 and 5 for 94, and England won by 5 wickets. He batted at number eleven, and when he joined R. E. Foster, who hit a record 287, the score was 447 for 9. They added 130 in 66 minutes, which remains the highest last wicket partnership by either side in England-Australia Test matches. Rhodes scored 40 not out.

In the second Test, in spite of having eight catches dropped off his bowling, Rhodes took 15 wickets for 124, and England won by 185 runs. His figures remain the best returned at Melbourne and were the best by an English bowler against Australia until 1934 when Verity took 15 for 104. Laker and Massie are the only bowlers to have improved on those figures.

England won the series by three matches to two. Rhodes took 31 wickets at 15·74, and, in the last Test, he opened the batting with Tom Hayward in the first innings. In England, in 1903, he had scored a thousand runs and completed the 'double' for the first time. In all, he was to achieve this all-round peak sixteen times in his career, a record that will never be beaten.

When he visited Australia for the second time in 1907–08 Rhodes averaged 48·89 with the bat, and on his third trip in 1911–12 he bowled only 62 overs without taking a wicket, but triumphed with the bat as opening partner to Jack Hobbs. He batted number four and number five in the first Test, but moved up to open the innings with the master from the second Test onwards; all four were won. They shared a partnership of 147 in the third Test, and in the fourth Test, with Hobbs scoring 178 and Rhodes 179, they began England's innings with a partnership of 323, which remains the record opening partnership for either side in the series.

His batting improved season by season because he learned what cricket taught him and, because he was determined to be proficient in every department of the game, he could field anywhere. He was not a batsman whom crowds would flock to see, but he accumulated runs with care and precision. He and Hobbs became renowned for their running between the wickets, for their ability to saunter singles which others would never have recognised. It was thought, understanding and application that made Wilfred Rhodes a batsman. Only thirteen men have scored more runs in first-class cricket, only eight men have taken more catches, and nobody has taken more wickets.

His batting, like his bowling, was meticulous. He placed his off-drive so that no fielder could reach it, just as he pitched the ball in a way that made the batsman hit it straight to the fielders as he had set them.

In 1914 he once more completed the 'double'. When county cricket resumed in 1919 he was 41 years old. He received offers to play league cricket, but he returned to Yorkshire and scored 1,237 runs and took 164 wickets. As concessions to his age he spun the ball less and batted with a more open-chested stance, but in terms of performance and reputation he was undiminished.

Australia overwhelmed England in three series between 1920 and 1925 so that when they arrived in England in 1926 it was to play a rubber of immense importance, for England had not won since 1911–12. The first four Tests were drawn, marred by the weather, so the final Test at The Oval in mid-August became a dramatic climax which gripped the whole nation. The game was to be played to a finish, and England had a new captain, Percy Chapman.

Rhodes and Hobbs had been co-opted on to the selection committee at the beginning of the season. The other selectors had sounded Rhodes about playing in the earlier Tests, but he said that they needed a younger man. He was, however, in splendid form during the year, the last in which he was to do the 'double'. At the meeting to choose the side for the vital, final Test, Pelham Warner spoke for the rest of the committee. 'Wilfred,' he said, 'we think that you should play. You are still the best left-handed bowler in England, and in a match that is to be played to a finish it is likely that we shall have rain at some time or other. You can still spin 'em, you know.'

'And your length,' added Perrin, 'is as good as ever.'

'Well, I can keep 'em there or thereabouts,' replied Rhodes. It is an answer that has been immortalised.

'And,' said Gilligan, 'you're making runs for Yorkshire.'

'I can get a few,' agreed Rhodes.

'And your fielding is all right,' said Hobbs.

'The farther I run, the slower I get,' answered Rhodes, but he agreed to play.

The Oval Test of 1926 has gone down in cricket history as one of the most famous of all encounters. England won by 289 runs. Rhodes batted number seven and scored an invaluable 28 as England were bowled out for 280. He began with three maidens when he was put on to bowl, in the third of which he deceived and bowled the 'unbowlable' Woodfull. He later accounted for Richardson, 2 for 35 in 25 overs, 15 of them maidens. Hobbs and Sutcliffe had a wonderful opening stand of 172; Rhodes made 14. Larwood gained the early breakthrough when Australia set out in search of 415. Then came Rhodes. He sent back Ponsford, Bardsley, Collins and Richardson, 20 – 9 – 44 – 4, and England regained the 'Ashes' amid scenes of unprecedented jubilation.

Chapman led his team on to the balcony to accept the adulation of the crowd. Rhodes was the last to appear, and when he did the applause doubled in volume. Thomson, his biographer, noted the occasion: 'For a long moment he stood there, seemingly unseeing, as though his thousands of admirers were not there. Finally, he smiled. That smile was in itself an achievement, for he did not smile too easily.' He had first played Test cricket before Larwood, Stevens and his captain, Percy Chapman, had been born.

He played county cricket for four more seasons. He was the brain behind whoever was leading the Yorkshire side, and it was apparent to many that, on occasions, Rhodes was doing all the directing and planning. He was never offered the Yorkshire captaincy, although it was offered to, and rejected by, another Yorkshire professional, Herbert Sutcliffe.

Rhodes's Test career did not end at The Oval in 1926. He played in the first Test series in the West Indies, 1929–30, and he ended the world's longest Test career, 31 years, 315 days, at Sabina Park, Kingston, Jamaica, on 10 April 1930. He was 52 years, 165 days old, the oldest man ever to appear in a Test match. He scored 8 not out and 11 not out, and his bowling figures were 20·5 – 12 – 17 – 1 and 24 – 13 – 22 – 1. He could still put 'em there or thereabouts.

He played 26 times in 1930, scored 418 runs and took 73 wickets. His last match for Yorkshire, against M.C.C. at Scarborough, saw him score 41 and help Wood revive the side's fortunes, and then, in the second M.C.C. innings, dismiss Haigh, Duleepsinhji and Hendren at a cost of 48 runs. He fought and played seriously to the very end.

He coached at Harrow School for five years, and then his sight began to fail. An operation came too late, and the last years of his life were spent in darkness. He still attended matches, and his comment was sought. He remained what he had been all his years, a man of dignity, honesty and integrity who accepted all without complaint. He was in his 96th year when he died, and he had been blind for 21 years.

Rhodes did not play cricket in a flippant manner. He was no gay cavalier of an all-rounder. He played cricket with seriousness and purpose at all times. He knew his worth and he gave of himself to the full in all circumstances. No man understood the game better. Rhodes could watch from the pavilion and, in mid-conversation, turn to his skipper when he noticed the twist a ball had taken and suggest it was time to declare. In one of the numerous stories about him, he is said to have inspected a rain-affected wicket with Emmott Robinson. 'That'll be turning by four o'clock,' said Robinson. 'Nay, Emmott,' said Wilf, '*half-past* four.'

In figures, Wilfred Rhodes is unquestionably the greatest all-rounder the game has seen since Grace, but then there was the exuberance of Hirst and the brief, dynamic glory of Jackson. If Yorkshire could find their like again, England would be rich indeed.

5

THE GOLDEN AGE OF THE COUNTY ALL-ROUNDER

When Hirst, Peel and Giffen did the 'double' in 1896 it was the first time that three cricketers had achieved the feat in the same season, and it brought the number of times that it had been accomplished to seventeen, Grace having accounted for seven of them. From 1897 until the outbreak of the Second World War, the 'double' was to become a common occurrence. On average, some six or seven players a season would achieve the mark, and in 1920, 1921, 1923 and 1930 the number was in double figures. At one time the all-rounder had been a cricketer of outstanding ability and accomplishment, a rare being; now he was an integral part of every county side.

The advent of Charles Lucas Townsend and Gilbert Jessop played some part in the Gloucestershire committee's rather cavalier treatment of W.G. Grace which caused him to move to Crystal Palace in 1899. Townsend was a right-arm slow bowler and left-handed batsman who achieved a notable hat trick against Somerset at Cheltenham in 1893 when wicket-keeper Brain stumped three successive batsmen. He became the first man after Grace to score two thousand runs and take a hundred wickets in a season, 1889, but he faded from the game at the beginning of the twentieth century, although he did hit 129 in two hours against the Australians in 1909.

His team-mate, Gilbert Jessop, succeeded Grace as Gloucestershire's captain. Jessop was a renowned, furious hitter whose fifty-three centuries came at the incredible rate of nearly 83 runs an hour. He was a quick bowler and he did the 'double' in 1897 and 1900, but, in truth, at the highest level, he was good enough neither as a batsman nor a bowler.

One of the best all-rounders in the early years of the twentieth century was Ted Arnold, who helped to raise Worcestershire to first-class status.

C. L. Townsend was the first cricketer to score two thousand runs and take a hundred wickets in a season after W. G. Grace, but he faded from the game at the beginning of the century.

Gilbert Jessop's powers as one of the greatest hitters the world has seen have tended to obscure the fact that he was also a very fine medium pace bowler.

He played an important part in the success of Warner's side in Australia in 1903–04 with his fast bowling which he varied intelligently. He was also a good batsman who could defend soundly and hit the ball hard, but he would never have been picked for England for his batting alone.

The same must also be said of Albert Edward Relf who performed the 'double' eight times and was one of the very best all-rounders in the years leading up to the First World War. He was already 25 years old when he joined Sussex from Norfolk in 1900. He was a medium pace bowler of relentless accuracy who could exploit a crumbling wicket to its fullest advantage, and he regularly finished high in the bowling averages. He never tired and he supported his colleagues' bowling with magnificent slip fielding. He accumulated more than twenty thousand runs in his career and hit 26 centuries, but he was not the most stylish of players. He played in thirteen Tests and performed quite well, but, in effect, he was the father of a great line of county all-rounders, the backbone of cricket, who were to give loyal and tireless service year after year until the game began to change in the 1960s.

Relf was a mainstay of the Sussex side until 1921 when he scored 753 runs, took 38 wickets, had a benefit and left first-class cricket at the age of 47. He became coach at Wellington College, and he was a happy and most popular man. He became wealthy and comfortable, but, tragically, he shot himself in a fit of depression brought on by an illness suffered by his wife.

In another age Relf may well have held a regular place in the England side, but he, like John Gunn, had to contend with Hirst, Rhodes and others. John Gunn played only six Test matches, and only one of them in England. He was a hard-working left-hander who scored more than twenty thousand runs and took more than a thousand wickets. He could hit hard and score fast and bowled a little quicker than most of the record books have given him credit for. He was one of a famous Nottinghamshire cricketing family who served the county well, but his great years were those of the Golden Age when there were giants in the land.

One of those giants should have been an Australian by the name of Albert Edwin Trott, but life overtook him and he ended in tragedy. 'Alberto' Trott made one of the most amazing debuts that Test cricket has known. He was chosen to play for Australia against England at Adelaide in January 1895. Batting at number ten, he hit 38 not out and 72 not out, bowled three overs for 9 runs in the first innings and in the second, bowling unchanged, took 8 for 43. Only two other bowlers, Valentine and Massie, have taken 8 wickets on their Test debut.

It was taken for granted that he would be in the Australian side which came to England in 1896 and was captained by his brother Harry, but, for reasons that were never disclosed, he was not selected. He had been seen as the most promising Australian cricketer of his generation, but, disenchanted by the treatment he had received, he came to England, joined the Lord's ground staff and qualified for Middlesex. He made his debut for them in 1898, but was handicapped by injury. In the next two seasons, however, he scored over a thousand runs and took more than two hundred wickets, the first man to accomplish this feat which, Hirst's unique double apart, has since been equalled by only Kennedy and Tate. To add to the three Tests he had played for Australia, he played twice for England, taking 17 wickets in his two Tests in South Africa in 1899.

His bowling was of exceptional variety. His arm was low, but he imparted a considerable amount of spin and could generate a fair pace. His yorker was bowled at a tremendous speed. His hitting was prodigious and his fielding brilliant. In 1899, playing for M.C.C. against the Australians, he hit a ball from Noble over the Pavilion at Lord's. Some said that he declined as a batsman from that point because he was ever trying to repeat the shot.

For two seasons at the turn of the century, Trott was the best all-rounder in the world, and a great career beckoned. The first tragedy was that he declined in skill so soon after reaching the highest point. He had a strong personality and he was immensely popular, but although he took 176 wickets and scored 880 runs in 1901 he was not quite the man he had been. He put on much weight and became muscle-bound so that he was no longer able to bowl the extra fast ball that had produced so many wickets, and after 1904 he was but a shadow of his former self. There was, however, to be one further flash of genius, and that came in his benefit match against Somerset at Lord's on Whit Monday 1907.

In Somerset's second innings he had Lewis l.b.w. and then bowled Poyntz, Woods and Robson with the next three deliveries. He finished the Somerset innings with another hat trick, having Mordaunt and Bailey caught and bowling Wickham. Four wickets in four balls and a hat trick in the same innings is a feat unparalleled in the history of cricket.

He ended his career with Middlesex in 1910 and became a first-class umpire, but ill-health forced him to give up, and in July 1914 came the greater tragedy when, perplexed by dropsy, he shot himself. He was in his 42nd year. He left his wardrobe to his landlady, and it was found that he possessed £4.

Albert Trott should have a place in this chronicle of great all-rounders,

Jack Gregory – fast bowler and a furious hitter. His partnership with McDonald as Australia's new ball opening pair devastated England in 1921.

but circumstances and a fatal flaw of character deemed otherwise, and he has left only a taste of a greatness that could have been.

His countryman, Frank Tarrant, misses greatness on another count. He came to England unknown, joined the Lord's ground staff and qualified to play for Middlesex as Trott had done. He had to overcome a great deal of hostility, for there was much adverse criticism about the importation of cricketers from Australia and elsewhere. He overcame this hostility by his joyful approach to the game although he was, by nature, a batsman who relied mainly on caution. He bowled left-arm slow-medium pace. He did the 'double' in 1907, when *Wisden* placed him ahead of Hirst and Rhodes, and in each of the seven seasons that followed up to the outbreak of war. Only Hirst did the 'double' more seasons in succession.

Had Tarrant stayed in Australia he must surely have become a Test cricketer, but as he was never tried at the highest level he must remain a model county professional all-rounder and no more.

Between the world wars he moved into horse-racing, buying and selling thoroughbreds in India and Australia, numbering princes among his friends and dying a wealthy man.

A third Australian, Herbie Collins, achieved the 'double' with the Australian Imperial Forces team in 1919, but the future Australian captain was to take only four wickets in Test cricket.

Jack Gregory, like Warwick Armstrong, did the 'double' in 1921. Gregory was McDonald's opening partner in a frightening new-ball pairing which destroyed England. He hit what was then the fastest century in Test cricket, in 70 minutes, against South Africa at Johannesburg in 1921, but his career was a short one, ended by injury in 1928.

The Gregory – McDonald combination had a devastating effect upon English batsmen in 1921, and Frank Woolley considered that the two best innings of his career were played against them for England at Lord's in that year when he hit 95 and 93. There are those who believe that the cricket field has never witnessed a finer sight than Frank Woolley. 'There was all summer in a stroke by Woolley,' said Robertson-Glasgow, following Cardus, 'and he batted as it is sometimes shown in dreams.'

He was a tall left-handed batsman for whom the term elegant is totally inadequate. He scored more runs in first-class cricket than any batsman bar Jack Hobbs, and he scored them at a rate exceeded only by Jessop and equalled only by Trumper. There was a fragile beauty in his batting which is not to say that he was vulnerable, but that the languid grace of his style suggested the mortality that makes humanity so precious. Tall and slender, quiet and charming, essentially calm, his batting was a fusion of elegance and power. The timing was perfect, and the power of driving tremendous. He never suggested a defence that was impenetrable because he was essentially an attacking player.

In 1934, at the age of 47, he won the Lawrence Trophy for the fastest century of the season, and in his last season, 1938, he took 81 in an hour off the Australians at Canterbury. He scored quickly and gloriously throughout his career, yet his back foot defence remained a model of perfection to the end. The historian, Arrowsmith, has suggested that he never played forward for defence, believing that a ball which could be played forward at all could be played with a full swing of the bat. He was upstanding, majestic, almost lackadaisical in command, exuding a thrilling beauty. Yet we have already fallen into the trap in talking about Woolley that we fall into when we talk about Grace or Sobers. The man was such a magnificent batsman that we forget, temporarily, that he has an undisputed place among the very narrow bracket of the greatest all-rounders that the world has known.

He was born in Tonbridge on 27 May 1887, and as a boy he haunted the Tonbridge ground which was, at the time, the Kent ground at which young players were groomed. His ability as a batsman and bowler attracted attention, and, in 1903, he was engaged to take part in morning practice and play occasionally in the afternoons if required. In 1904 he was taken on to the ground staff at Tonbridge, and in 1906 he made his debut in first-class cricket.

From the moment of his first appearance he was recognised as a very good slow left-arm bowler. He played his first game for Kent against Lancashire at Old Trafford, batted number eight, scored 0 and 64, and took the wicket of Hornby at a personal cost of 103 runs. His second match was against Somerset at Gravesend. Kent gained a notable victory when Somerset collapsed before his spin in the second innings. He finished with 6 for 39.

1906 was to be a memorable year for Kent for they won the county championship for the first time. They had lost to Yorkshire and Lancashire, drawn with Essex, and beaten Sussex and Somerset in their opening matches so that they were not seen as title contenders by mid-June. 'The turning point came in the match against Surrey at The Oval, on June 14 and 15,' wrote *Wisden*. 'Kent entered upon the game under a serious disadvantage, a damaged hand keeping Blythe away, but after a tremendous fight they won by one wicket. The colt, Woolley, regarded for some little time as the most promising of the young professionals at the Tonbridge nursery, had the chief share in the victory, and made his name both as a bowler and a batsman. No sterner game was seen during the whole summer.'

Surrey were all out for 73 in less than an hour and a half on the first day. Woolley had begun the rot by clean bowling three of the first four batsmen, Hayward, Hayes and Goatly. Kent struggled in their turn, and they were 61 for 6 before Woolley joined Hubble. The young left-hander made 72 out of a stand of 101 in 65 minutes, and Kent took a first innings lead of 127.

Hayes and Hobbs nearly pulled the game round for Surrey, but Woolley bowled Hayes for 84, went on to take 5 for 82, and Kent were left to make 128 to win. They lost half their side for 66, and eight men were out for 99. When Fairservice was caught behind off Lees, who bowled splendidly, Kent were still 19 short of victory with one wicket only remaining. Fielder joined Woolley, and the runs were obtained. Woolley finished on 23 not out. Three years later, at Stourbridge, Woolley and Fielder were to put on 235 for the last wicket against Worcestershire, and this remains an English record.

Frank Woolley celebrated the triumph over Surrey at The Oval by taking 8 Hampshire wickets for 57 runs in the next match at Tonbridge. He also hit 116, his maiden first-class century. He was to hit 145 hundreds in his career, which places him seventh in the list, and of those above him only Wally Hammond bowled with any seriousness.

He ended that first season with 779 runs and 42 wickets, and although his bowling had to give way later in the year to Blythe, on whom he had modelled himself, it was apparent that an all-rounder of exceptional talent had arrived.

His arrival coincided with a golden period in Kent cricket history, for they won the title again in 1909, 1910 and 1913. Woolley achieved the first of his eight 'doubles' in 1910, and he was to accomplish the feat six seasons in succession from 1914 onwards. Four times in a season he topped two thousand runs and took more than a hundred wickets. No cricketer has equalled this record. J.W. Hearne did it three times, Hirst and Rhodes twice.

John William Hearne was a fine all-round cricketer who batted soundly and bowled leg-breaks and googlies to great effect in county cricket, although less successfully at Test level. He was a stalwart of the Middlesex side, but his career, marred by ill-health, was blighted by the First World War which came when he was at his best.

It can be said that Woolley, too, lost some of his best years to the war, for he was 27 when war broke out and was an established Test cricketer.

Frank Woolley. Tall and elegant as a batsman; intelligent and cunning as a bowler.

Yet the war years seemed not to harm him, for in the three seasons, 1920 to 1922, he scored 6,047 runs, only once failing to reach two thousand, and then by only 76 runs, and took 515 wickets, exceeding 160 in each of the three years.

However much his batting was to dominate in later years, it must be remembered that it was as an all-round player that he was picked for the representative elevens of 1911 and 1912. He first played for England against Australia at The Oval in 1909. It was the last Test of the series. He was then chosen for every England side until the end of 1926, and played 52 Test matches in succession.

In South Africa, 1909–10, and Australia, 1911–12, his bowling was used sparingly, but still, on occasions, effectively. In the last Test of Douglas's side's 'Ashes' triumph of 1911–12, he hit 133 not out, the first Test century by an English left-hander against Australia, and shared a seventh wicket partnership of 143 with Vine, a record for England against Australia. Frank Woolley hit five Test hundreds.

In that Sydney Test he also took 2 for 1 and 1 for 36, and in the Triangular Tournament in England in 1912 he took 5 for 41 and 1 for 24, and 5 for 29 and 5 for 20 in successive Tests against South Africa and Australia. Surprisingly, his best bowling performance in a Test match was to come as late as January 1930, when he took 7 for 76 against New Zealand at Wellington. Mills and Dempster had put on 276 for New Zealand's first wicket. Woolley was the sixth bowler tried, and he dismissed them both.

He bowled less and less after being hampered by a knee injury sustained in Australia in 1924, but even in his last two seasons, 1937 and 1938, he took 31 and 22 wickets respectively, and at Oakham in August 1938, a month before his retirement at the age of 51, he took 5 for 49 and 6 for 57 as Kent beat Leicestershire.

'Elegant and dashing left-handed batsman – best in execution and as an attractive personality whom we have known during thirty years – Woolley announced his decision to retire and on every ground he received a very affectionate farewell, each county team and their supporters clearly demonstrating their appreciation of one of the finest players who have graced the game.' *Wisden*'s comment echoed the general feeling. He reached a thousand runs for the season as he had done every year since 1907, his second in the Kent eleven, and he captained the Players at Lord's.

His last game was for England Past and Present against Sir Pelham Warner's XI in the Folkestone Festival. He scored 22 and 31, and he caught Jack Robertson at slip off Wilkinson. He took 1,018 catches in his career, mostly at slip, and Grace's 872 is a long way behind as the second in the list. As one of his county colleagues said: 'Nobody was ever bored by what Frank Woolley did or said on a cricket field!'

He is the second leading run-maker in the history of the game. He is one of thirty odd bowlers who have passed two thousand first-class wickets, but of those only W.G. Grace has also reached 40,000 runs. Nobody has taken as many catches. He scored more than three thousand Test runs and took 83 Test wickets. Yet his figures do not tell half the story, for it was the manner of achievement that was his greatness. If some have hesitated to place him among the very geatest all-rounders, it is only because the memory of the liquid grace of his batting has tended to dim the mind to all else.

If the batting of Woolley has tended to obscure the quality of his bowling, then the bowling of Maurice Tate has hidden from later generations the fact that here was an all-rounder who reached the double mark of a thousand runs and a hundred wickets in 33 Test matches, and the only other Englishman to have reached the mark more quickly is Ian Botham. Yet, as he passes further back into history, the fact that he once opened the innings for England against Australia, that he hit a Test century, that he scored 21,717 runs, did the 'double' eight times and hit 23 first-class hundreds becomes hazier and hazier. 'That he was a very serviceable batsman who, on occasions, opened the innings for his county and 12 times scored a thousand runs in a season, is often overlooked,' wrote Ian Peebles. 'But this was a small matter in comparison with the glory of Tate in his opening overs at Hove on a green wicket, freshened by a slight sea haze.'

That was the whole point with Tate. He was unarguably the greatest fast-medium pace bowler of his era. That he was a more than competent batsman was a bonus, but it was also an irrelevance.

He was the son of an honest Sussex medium pace off-break bowler who played once for England. Poor Fred Tate's Test was a disaster. At Old Trafford, in 1902, he was preferred to the great George Hirst, much to general annoyance, dropped a vital catch and was bowled when England were only 4 runs short of victory. Legend has it that on the train journey back south after the match he turned to Len Braund and said, 'I've got a little lad there at home who'll make it up for me.' The little lad did.

Maurice Tate was engaged on the Sussex ground staff in 1910, and he first played for Sussex as a slow-medium off-break bowler, like his father, in 1912, but his progress until the outbreak of the First World War was slow and unexceptional. He returned from the war physically harder and a little thicker in the frame so that he received the nickname that his father had also been given, 'Chub'. There was a doubt in the Sussex club as to whether he should be re-engaged, but the age of Albert Relf and George Cox made it necessary for Sussex to encourage some younger players, and Tate was offered a contract.

The improvement in his play continued to be slow, and he seemed destined to follow his father as being nothing more than a good county professional, honest in endeavour, but uninspiring in achievement. He forced his way up the batting order and, in 1921, against Northamptonshire at Hove, he and Ted Bowley put on a record 385 for the Sussex second wicket. More significantly, he began to develop a quicker ball. One observer remarked that it was Ernest Tyldesly who was first bowled by it and suggested to Tate that he should concentrate on bowling fast-medium pace; John Arlott places the formidable Philip Mead as Tate's decisive victim. He fell to Tate in the Sussex–Hampshire game at Eastbourne, at the end of July 1922.

'The bowler in those days had in Mead one of the most discouraging opponents. His eye and judgement were alike almost perfect: he saw no reason to hurry and he played with such deliberation as to imply impregnability. Tate swung all his body into bowling Mead a quicker ball and, almost inadvertently, bowled him a cutter. The ball pitched on the left-hander's off stump and hit the top of the leg stump like a rifle bullet. Mead gave the bowler a dry and slightly surprised look as he walked out but, in his usual manner, said nothing, for he was never a man to encourage bowlers by word or sign. Philip Mead on that July day was dismissed by the first ball bowled in a manner destined to make cricket history even greater than the Hampshire man's batting.'

For the next three seasons, Maurice Tate took over two hundred wickets and scored over a thousand runs. No one else has achieved this feat three times. In effect, Maurice Tate fathered modern seam bowling. He held the ball with the seam between and parallel to his first two fingers, and he swerved the ball from leg frighteningly late. He was not particularly quick through the air, but all who played against him swore, what scientists deny is possible, that he gained pace from the pitch. Certainly this seemed to be the case in Australia.

His Test debut was against South Africa at Edgbaston in 1924. It was sensational. He dismissed Susskind with his first ball in Test cricket, went on to take 4 for 12, and South Africa were all out for 30, only 19 runs coming from the bat. In the fifth Test of the same series he scored his first Test fifty.

In Australia, the following winter, England were beaten 4–1, but Tate took 38 wickets, a record which was later bettered first by Bedser and then by Laker. In the years between the two world wars, Maurice Tate was the most successful of England bowlers in matches against Australia, 19 wickets ahead of Harold Larwood.

From 1922 to 1929, he completed the 'double' every season, thus equalling Tarrant's performance. They were years rich in county all-rounders, but none could match Tate's consistency.

Strong shoulders, big feet, brisk, easy action, and an elastic delivery, Tate bowled with his heart as well as his head. He enjoyed every moment of his cricket. He was a fun-maker and a friend-maker, and had the zest that one associates with the great all-rounder.

His stamina was limitless. 'It is a great point in his favour,' said *Wisden*, citing him as one of the five cricketers of the year in the 1924 edition, 'that, thanks to his beautiful delivery, he can get through a lot of work without undue fatigue.' The same essay also gave a clue as to the reason for later historians ignoring his claims as a batsman. 'Tate is a good, free-hitting batsman, capable at any time of getting his fifty runs, but one hopes that for the next few years, at least, the lure of long scores will not attract him. With heavy tasks ahead for English cricket his business is to take wickets.'

There's the rub. England were strong in batting. They had need of Tate for his bowling. In effect, they were saying to Tate what Lord Hawke had said to Wilfred Rhodes, 'Now, Wilfred (Maurice), no more than twenty.'

All appraisals of Tate emphasise the greatness of his bowling; few speak of his batting. Yet he is one of only seven English cricketers to have achieved the 'double' in Test cricket, and his overall record as an all-rounder places him firmly in the very highest class. Arlott recalls that figures can tell one nothing of his batting. 'They cannot tell of its power and gaiety and how it often saved a game and how we warmed to the sight of him lurching in to the wicket at a friendly roll, wriggling his pads comfortably, his bat cocked from a grip close to the handle and with a word to the fieldsman and umpire on the way.'

Watching Maurice Tate play cricket was a fine thing, and 'it set a thrill inside the chest like fine music'. All remember him with love. It is likely that he would never have been picked to play for England for his batting alone, but that part of his ability was allowed to wither somewhat because his country had need of him in another role.

One of the reasons that Sussex offered Tate a contract after the war was because Vallance Jupp, their leading all-rounder, had decided to turn amateur. In 1921, he was to leave them and he became secretary/captain of Northamptonshire.

It is probable that many followers of the game, approaching a study of great all-rounders, would be well acquainted with the names of Hirst, Rhodes, Tate and Woolley, but the inclusion of one, V.W.C. Jupp, may well surprise them. Some facts are, therefore, in order.

Vallance Jupp completed the 'double' for Sussex in 1920, and he repeated the feat the following year when he scored 2,169 runs and took 121 wickets. Only thirteen players have scored two thousand runs and taken a hundred wickets in a season. With the exception of 1929, he achieved the 'double' for Northamptonshire every season from 1925 to 1933. His ten 'doubles' have been bettered only by Rhodes, sixteen, and Hirst, fourteen. He and Freddie Brown are the only cricketers to have done the 'double' for two different counties, Surrey, 1932 and Northamptonshire, 1949. He is one of only nine cricketers to have scored a century and done the hat trick in the same match, for Sussex against Essex at Colchester in 1921. In all, he did the hat trick five times, which places him behind Doug Wright, seven, and Charlie Parker and Tom Goddard, six. When he was named as one of *Wisden*'s five cricketers of the year in 1928 he was in august company, for Hammond and Jardine were among the chosen. He was considered the best amateur all-rounder of his day, which places him above J.W.H.T. Douglas and Percy Fender.

Douglas was a tough player and resolute man. He was a fine, natural, fast-medium bowler, but he was a self-made batsman, the product of application and relentless determination.

Of Fender myths have grown. It is argued that he should have captained England, for he was such an intelligent captain of Surrey, and it has been suggested that the reasons that he was never chosen as England's captain were anti-semitic. He was a furiously aggressive batsman, who hit one of the fastest centuries on record, 35 minutes, a good leg-break bowler and a fine fielder, but his international record was moderate, and inferior to Jupp's. He accomplished the 'double' six times in the 1920s, however, and, in one of his several excellent books, *The Turn of the Screw*, which dealt with the 1928–29 England tour of Australia, hinted that he felt he should have been chosen for that side. He was also quite dismissive of Don Bradman.

Jupp had fewer pretensions. Born in Burgess Hill in Sussex in 1891, he was educated privately before going to St John's School where his cricketing prowess attracted the attention of the Sussex committee. He joined Sussex as a professional, made rapid improvement and hit 217 not out against Worcestershire at Worcester in 1914. He topped 1,500 runs and took 51 wickets with his medium pace. He was recognised as an all-rounder of outstanding merit.

When war broke out he joined the Royal Engineers, served in France, Salonika and Palestine, transferred to the Royal Air Force as a cadet and was demobilised in July 1919. He played the rest of that season as an amateur for Sussex, having decided to earn a living in business. His qualities as a cricketer had increased rather than diminished although his bowling had now become off-spin. He turned the ball considerably.

Short, prematurely bald, with broad shoulders, long arms and a rough humour, Jupp was selected to tour Australia in 1920–21, but he could not make the trip because of his business interests. He first played for England in that sorry, haphazard summer of 1921. He was included in the side for the first and third Tests, and with 5 for 142 and 65 runs in four innings, he did as well as anybody, but that was a year of selection vagaries.

He moved his business to Northampton, qualified for the county by residence and became secretary. He was captain from 1927 to 1931 although it was a position about which he was never too keen. He accepted the invitation to tour South Africa with Freddie Mann's side in 1922–23, played in four Tests and bowled with considerable success in the first one. His only other two Tests were against West Indies in 1928. His 28 Test wickets cost him 22 runs each, an excellent return at that period, but he was less successful with the bat, managing 208 runs, average 17·33.

As a batsman, he was by nature a player of great energy, scoring with freedom and driving fiercely, but he was able to defend with extreme care when the occasion demanded. His off-breaks were bowled with a rolling gait. 'His physical resemblance to a typical French abbé was gradually enhanced by a tendency to rotundness; he assumed responsibility with bland negligence in his merry fashion, but tossed up slows with beguiling gumption and could bat with resolute aggressiveness.'

In 1932 he took all ten Kent wickets at Tunbridge Wells, and he played with merit in a very weak Northamptonshire side until 1938. He was one of the best players in England between the two world wars, and he was a splendid all-rounder. That he was not a great one was most probably because it did not matter quite enough to him.

The only all-rounders who could rival Jupp in achievement in the inter-war years were Ewart Astill of Leicestershire and Morris Nichols of Essex. Astill never played Test cricket against Australia, but with George

Geary, he carried Leicestershire for two decades. He was an orthodox right-handed batsman and a bowler who could spin the ball both ways. He was a delightful man, on and off the field. He was a billiards player of considerable accomplishment and a musician who entertained his colleagues with song, piano and banjo. He played cricket from 1906 to 1939, and he did the 'double' nine times between 1921 and 1930. He played in the five Tests in South Africa, 1928–29, and in the four in the West Indies, 1929–30, but, in truth, these selections were recognition of him as an honest, county professional whose life was cricket. The winter of 1928 was the only one in seven years in which he did not find himself engaged in a tour of some sort.

Morris Stanley Nichols had a richer Test career although he commanded a regular place in the England side only in the 1935 series against South Africa. He played only once for England against Australia, at Old Trafford, in 1930, when he took 2 for 33 in 21 overs and scored 7 not out. Inexplicably, he was not picked for the next Test even though England needed him, and he suffered an even greater misfortune in 1938 when, selected in the party for the third Test against Australia at Old Trafford which was abandoned without a ball being bowled, he was not chosen again during the series. Nevertheless, his fourteen Tests brought him 355 runs and 41 wickets.

He was a fast right-arm bowler and a left-handed batsman who could hit the ball very hard indeed. He performed the 'double' eight times between 1929 and 1939. He was modest in demeanour and sleek in appearance, his hair brushed flat and parted in the centre. It was his custom to pack his dancing pumps with his cricket kit when the county were on tour so that he could follow his other interest in the evenings.

In the days when the county championship was the only tournament for which the first-class counties competed, and that was monopolised by Yorkshire, he produced the outstanding all-round performance which took his county, Essex, to victory over the all-conquering white rose county. Until the heady days which followed 1979, it was the most memorable victory in Essex cricket history, and it is still the one most talked about.

The Yorkshire side which took the field at the Fartown Ground, Huddersfield, on 31 July and 1 August 1935, contained eight players who had played or were to play for England. Yorkshire had not been beaten since August of the previous year. The home county batted first, and in less than an hour they were all out for 31. Read and Nichols bowled unchanged. Nichols took 4 for 17. Essex began badly and were 39 for 4 when Nichols came in. Rist, who had opened, stayed with him until the score reached 65, and then he fell to Verity. Nichols was now joined by B.H. Belle, a young amateur who made infrequent appearances and was later to captain Suffolk. They added 174. Nichols laid about the Yorkshire attack in magnificently aggressive fashion. He made 146 before being caught by Hutton off Bowes, and Essex were all out for 334 at close of play on the first day.

Yorkshire began their second innings on the Thursday morning, and the match was over by one o'clock. Nichols bowled unchanged and took 7 for 37. He had bowled Hutton for 0 in the first innings, and he had him l.b.w. for 0 in the second. He claimed Sutcliffe twice, for 4 and 1. Yorkshire were out for 99, and Essex won by an innings and 204 runs.

He was a marvellous trier, and he never admitted defeat. Sir Home Gordon, in one of his more perceptive passages, reached an accurate assessment of Nichols who, in an era of good all-rounders, was one of the very best.

'Never can I recollect a greater trier than Stan Nichols. No matter how long or how hot the day, he never flags, is never ruffled, always playing in high spirits and in the right spirit. It does not seem to be realised why, though so excellent a bowler, he has never become even greater. The explanation is that he is flat-footed and, try as he has ever so hard, he can never get onto his toes at the moment of delivering the ball, thus losing just that extra little bit of nip which is so devastating. He is well aware of this himself, and has discussed the matter with me. In a county match, if I had to have one man to play for me to save my life, pre-War it would have been George Hirst, post-War it would be Stan Nichols.'

This was written on the eve of the outbreak of the Second World War which brought to an end the great era of the county all-rounder.

Somerset had Bill Andrews, one of cricket's richest characters and loveliest of men, and Arthur Wellard, who hit more sixes in a season than anyone until Botham came along. Hampshire had Alec Kennedy, and Derbyshire had Stan Worthington, George Pope and Leslie Townsend.

Two Middlesex amateurs who captained England, Walter Robins and 'Gubby' Allen, were among the finest all-rounders of their generation. Robins was an ebullient cricketer, an exciting batsman and a leg-spinner of variety and invention. He was a brilliant fielder and an inspiring captain who brightened every game in which he played. G.O. Allen, knighted for his services to cricket in 1986, was a fast bowler and a sound batsman, but the time that he could give to cricket was limited, and one can only

Walter Hammond. He was England's finest batsman in succession to Hobbs, and he was also an excellent medium pace bowler and a slip fielder second to none.

69

conjecture how great an all-rounder he may have been had the game occupied his time fully.

There was, however, one figure who dominated all other Englishmen in the years between 1928 and 1939, and that was Wally Hammond. He was the greatest batsman that England had seen after Jack Hobbs, and his 167 centuries, 22 of them in Tests, are proof of that. To have watched Hammond bat and seen that exquisite cover drive is a gift for which one should remain eternally grateful, but the sheer majesty, assurance and beauty of his batting, as with Woolley, has tended to dim the fact that he was a medium-pace bowler with an easy, flowing action. He had a command of length and late swing which brought him 732 first-class wickets, 83 of them in Test matches. Added to this, he was, in the opinion of most people, the best slip fielder that the game has known. Neville Cardus in an obituary in *Wisden* wrote: 'He gave the impression of relaxed carelessness. At the first sight, or hint of, a snick off the edge, his energy swiftly concentrated in him, apparently electrifying every nerve and muscle in him. He became light, boneless, airborne. He would take a catch as the ball was travelling away from him, leaping to it as gracefully as a trapeze artist to the flying trapeze.'

The tributes to him after his death inevitably touched upon his position as one of the greatest batsmen in the history of the game, but none failed to mention his outstanding ability as a bowler. Alec Bedser was adamant that he was the greatest all-rounder he had ever known. His Gloucestershire colleague Charlie Barnett considered him the greatest athlete he had ever known, and Bill Bowes remarked that he was a naturally gifted player of all games. Tom Goddard said that he was a brilliant bowler and an incomparable fielder. Stan McCabe of Australia, himself an all-rounder of quality, said of Hammond, 'Everything he did, he did with the touch of a master. One could refer to him as the perfect cricketer.' Alan Melville, the South African and Sussex captain, stated that Hammond was the greatest all-rounder that he ever played against.

These may seem exaggerated claims for one who between 1927 and 1950 only twice averaged under 55 a season and topped 50 wickets in a season on only four occasions. In the inter-war years, however, in the matches against Australia, the hardest and most meaningful test, he was England's leading all-rounder by a mile, was seventh among the bowlers and second only to Sutcliffe, by 57 runs, as the most prolific England run-scorer. Only Bradman topped them on the Australian side.

His early years were frustrated by illness and by the necessity to qualify for Gloucestershire as Kent, knowing he was born in Dover, had raised objections. At first he was ignored by England selectors because they considered him too rash in his stroke play, ever the conservatives, and he missed the whole of the 1926 season, when he was needed, through illness. In 1927 he emulated W.G. Grace by scoring a thousand runs in May. His Test debut came in South Africa the following winter, but the world was stunned by his achievements in Australia in 1928–29. He scored 905 runs in five Tests, an England record. He was to hit nine centuries against Australia between 1928 and 1938, and four of them were double centuries.

So great were the demands on his batting that his bowling was not used as much as it might have been, but he opened the England bowling with Tate in three Tests in South Africa, 1930–31, and at Adelaide, 1936–37, he took 5 Australian wickets, including that of Bradman, for 57 runs in an innings of 433.

He turned amateur in 1938 and captained England that year, the following year and immediately after the Second World War. He was troubled by lumbago and personal problems on the tour to Australia, 1946–47, and did not play in the last Test, by then he had virtually ceased to bowl.

His records were legion: 227 and 336 not out in successive innings against New Zealand; 10 catches in a match for Gloucestershire against Surrey; 819 catches in his career. His quality as a bowler cannot be measured by figures alone; like Woolley had he been a lesser batsman, he could have given more to his bowling.

While his cricket remained unruffled, immaculate and poised, his personality was often withdrawn, taciturn to the point of moroseness. He retired from the game which he had adorned so splendidly, lost his capital in an unwise venture, drank heavily, strained personal relationships and moved to South Africa where he was employed as coach-groundsman at Natal University. He died in 1962, somewhat impoverished and a rather sad figure of a faded star, but to those who saw him he left a warm glow which they will always cherish.

Wally Hammond played 85 times for England; Jim Parks played only once. He played for Sussex as a brave, solid right-handed opening batsman, medium pace in-swing bowler and excellent fielder from 1924 to 1939. In 1937 he hit 3,003 runs and took 101 wickets. One can safely suggest that this record will remain unique in the annals of cricket. The magnitude of the achievement could not be ignored by the Test selectors, and he was chosen to play for England against New Zealand in the first match at Lord's.

His opening partner in that match was also making his Test debut. His name was Len Hutton and he scored 0 and 1. Jim Parks made 22 and 7, and he bowled well, taking 2 for 26 and 1 for 10 in the limited opportunity given to him. Hutton went on to greatness, and Parks was never picked again. Such is the way of the world.

His son was to play Test cricket, and his grandson has proved to be a very fine wicket-keeper for Hampshire. In truth, Jim Parks senior was essentially a county player, immensely dependable, but lacking the touch of genius which marks a Hammond, a Tate or a Woolley. He stamped his name boldly, however, on what was the golden age of the county all-rounder, when the 'double' had become a regular occurrence and the cricketer who could both bat and bowl to advantage was an integral part of every county side.

6

BARNACLE AND THE ENGLISH RENAISSANCE

The Second World War changed much, but not all of the changes that it was to bring about in cricket were to come in the first decade of peace. The late 1940s and early 1950s witnessed simply an exciting revival of what had been happening in 1938 and 1939. It was back to business as usual, but, initially at least, the boom in all-rounders appeared to have ceased. In 1939 Howorth, Martin and Nichols had been the leading all-rounders in the country; in 1946 Dick Howorth, the Worcestershire left-hander, was the only Englishman to complete the 'double'.

It is probable that Howorth lost his best years to the war, for he was 37 when first-class cricket resumed in 1946. England looked to a younger man, Jack Ikin, for the all-rounder's spot in the first Test after the war, and then turned to two older men, James Langridge and Peter Smith, both of them among the least lucky of cricketers.

James Langridge was a genuine all-rounder, a solid left-handed batsman and a slow left-arm bowler of the highest calibre. He and his brother John were backbones of the Sussex side for nearly thirty years, and James was captain from 1950 to 1952. He scored a thousand runs in a season on twenty occasions and did the 'double' six times in the 1930s. One of those 'doubles' came in 1933, and he completed it while making his Test debut for England, taking 7 for 56 in the second innings against West Indies at Old Trafford in 1933. He had a successful tour of India the following winter, scoring 70 at Calcutta, but he could never command a regular place in the England side because of the presence of Hedley Verity as the left-arm spinner. Verity was killed in the war, and James Langridge was recalled for the last Test against India in 1946 and selected for the tour of Australia that followed, but the years had rolled by, and it was too late, and he did not play in a Test in Australia.

Peter Smith earned his four Test matches. He was at a cinema in

Chelmsford in 1933 when a message was flashed on the screen telling him to report to the box office. He was told that he must go at once to The Oval as he had been called up for the Test match. When he arrived there he learned that he had been the victim of a hoax. He did not play Test cricket until the Oval Test against India in 1946 when he was 38. He toured Australia the following winter, took 9 for 121 in the first innings against New South Wales and played in two Tests. He also played in the Test match in New Zealand, and the following year did the 'double' for the only time. The most remarkable achievement by this leg-break bowler and judiciously aggressive batsman came in that year, 1947, when, although usually a middle-order batsman, he found himself at number eleven in the Essex side against Derbyshire at Chesterfield. He and Frank Vigar put on 218 for the last wicket, and T.P.B. Smith hit 163, the highest score ever made by a number eleven in first-class cricket. But still England searched for an all-rounder.

Dick Howorth at last got his chance at The Oval in 1947 when England drew with South Africa. He took the wicket of Dyer with his first ball in Test cricket, had match figures of 6 for 149 in a high-scoring game and scored 23 and 45 not out. He bore the brunt of the work when an unwisely weak England side was sent to the West Indies in 1947–48, and he did creditably. He took 6 for 124 in the second innings of the first Test, his victims including Stollmeyer, Walcott and Gomez, but that tour marked the end of his Test career.

There was a brief show of promise from Vincent Broderick of Northamptonshire, and a defiant revival by Freddie Brown, but the most consistent and dominant all-rounders were Australian importations – Walsh, Jackson, McCool, Dooland, Tribe and later Alley.

In 1949, however, a young Yorkshireman caused great excitement. It was his first season in first-class cricket, and he scored 1,098 runs and took 113 wickets. His name was Brian Close. He was 18 years old, the youngest player ever to achieve the 'double' and the only one to do it in the season of his first appearance in first-class cricket. He was whisked into the Test team to play against New Zealand at Old Trafford. He got the wicket of Wallace with a full toss and was out for 0.

National service limited his opportunities over the next two seasons, but he went to Australia with F.R. Brown's team in 1950–51. He became the youngest player to appear in the England–Australia matches, but he was not a success, neither was it a profitable tour in the cricketing sense. It was described rather unkindly by one critic as a party of 'spivs and schoolboys'.

In 1952 Close scored 1,192 runs and took 114 wickets, but it was to be the last time that he did the 'double'. His cricket was not aided by his excursion into professional football, and the promise was to remain largely unfulfilled. His Test career spanned 27 years, but he played only 22 Tests, failed to score a test century and took only 18 wickets. He was a brilliant close to the wicket fielder, and his courage was total. He was frighteningly fearless, and brought this unflinching bravery to his batting.

Recalled to the England Test side in 1963 to cope with the fearsome fast bowling of Hall and Griffith, he played a memorable innings of 70 at Lord's when England finished six short of victory with one wicket standing and Cowdrey at the crease with a broken arm in plaster. Yet even this innings caused controversy. Many accused him of throwing his wicket away with a rash shot, but he maintained he was forced to charge at Griffith and Hall because of the West Indies' slow over-rate and delaying tactics. Two years earlier, against Australia, he earned the wrath of spectators and selectors alike with a leg side clout at Benaud in the Old Trafford Test which cost him his wicket and, arguably, cost England the match.

These dismissals were uncharacteristic of the man, but the controversy that surrounded them was not. He became a tough and successful captain of Yorkshire and England, but he lost both positions because of disagreement. He ended as a very successful captain of Somerset where he gave early encouragement to a young Ian Botham. He later served as a Test selector. He was always liked and respected by those with whom he played.

He was a strong, left-handed batsman, sound in defence and capable of some very big hitting. He bowled right-arm medium pace or off-breaks, and therein lies one of the reasons that his talents as an all-rounder were never realised, for in his bowling he never really determined what sort of bowler he was, and he ended not being good enough at either.

As a character and a captain he has been one of the richest to grace the game; as an all-rounder he must rank as one of the greatest of disappointments at the top level although he might argue that, with his annual excursions at the Scarborough Festival, he still has time to prove himself. He is always one to argue his point with humour and conviction. He recently protested that he had been fined for speeding when he was barely travelling above seventy on the M1. He failed to mention that he was towing a caravan at the time.

One of the problems that attends Close, and others of his and following generations, is that increased radio and television coverage of the game has tended to emphasise or caricature certain aspects of personality and so distort a truer or fairer picture. Trevor Bailey has certainly suffered in this respect from the time that he was dubbed 'Barnacle'. The nickname was given in affection for his steadfast and heroic defence in batting which saved England in many a crisis, but to believe that his talents were restricted to the negation of the opposition is to miss ninety per cent of his charm and quality. He is one of the two all-rounders of real quality that England has seen since the war, and no man adapted himself better to the demands of any situation.

Under the guidance of Denys Wilcox who led Essex before the war, Trevor Bailey was an outstanding cricketer at his preparatory school, Alleyn Court, Westcliff-on-Sea. His promise continued at Dulwich, but he was 16 when war broke out so that important formative years could never have been so easy or so productive as they would have been in a more stable era. He headed both the batting and bowling averages at Dulwich in 1939, but *Wisden* commented that he 'could with profit have made more use of his attacking strokes'. Two years later, he scored 851 runs, averaged 121 for Dulwich and took 41 wickets, but G.H.M. Cartwright, in *Wisden*, saw him mainly as a batsman, noting that he 'bowled a lot and got wickets, but his bowling, useful though it is, cannot be considered in the same class as his batting, which is outstanding both in technique and execution'. He was, indeed, 'the best bat of the year' and 'an all-round player of outstanding ability'.

Cartwright continued his plaudits for Bailey's batting and his scepticism regarding his bowling in his public school notes in *Wisden* 1942: 'Bailey is a correct, quick-footed and attractive batsman of considerable variety of stroke, and, good bowler though he undeniably is, I feel that he would be well advised to make his batting his first concern.' As the young man had taken 66 wickets at 6·16 runs each and established a Dulwich College record, this advice seemed rather harsh. He was, too, proving himself at a higher level, appearing for the British Empire XI, a team of county and international players, in several of the charity games in which they regularly engaged and taking 4 for 36 for Middlesex & Essex against Kent & Surrey at Lord's.

The match was drawn with Middlesex & Essex finishing four short of victory with 6 wickets standing. Eight-ball overs were bowled and the game was played on 3 and 4 August 1942. *Wisden* was in ecstasies about Bailey's contribution: 'Trevor Bailey, the Dulwich College captain, put enthusiasm into a Bank Holiday crowd of 22,000 people – 16,693 paid for admission – by dismissing three batsmen in his first over. G.O. Allen gave way at 33 to Bailey, whose second ball beat Bennett; Ames hit 3 to the on, but the seventh delivery got Bridger leg-before and the next sent Todd's middle stump flying.'

He joined the Royal Marines, and he became a great favourite at Lord's in 1943 and 1944. His zestful approach ignited every game in which he played, and his wavy black hair was prominent whenever runs were being scored or wickets being taken. He was playing alongside the best – Edrich, Ames, Wright, Wyatt, Compton, Robins, Constantine – and he was more than holding his own.

Rather surprisingly, he played in none of the Victory 'Test' matches in 1945 although young, less well known, players – Donald Carr, John Dewes and the Hon. Luke White – were all given an outing. He served in Europe after D-Day and, on demobilisation, taught at his old preparatory school, Alleyn Court, where Denys Wilcox was headmaster, before going up to Cambridge in the autumn of 1946. In effect, the war had put back his cricket career by five years, although one should point out that at this time he was more committed to the idea of teaching as a profession rather than cricket.

His first game for Essex was at Ilford, in May 1946. Put in to bat on a damp wicket, Essex made 441 for 7 declared. Bailey opened and scored 39 and then took 5 Derbyshire wickets for 34. When Derbyshire followed-on he took 3 for 118, and Essex won by 8 wickets. It was the start of a happy and profitable association.

In 1946 he was not considered for any of the Test matches, nor did he play in any representative games, and with England desperately searching for a pace bowler and an all-rounder of quality, that is surprising.

At Cambridge, he flourished. He took not out centuries off the bowling of Yorkshire and Gloucestershire, two of the best attacks in the country, finished with 566 runs and took 49 wickets. He played ten times for Essex in the second half of the 1947 season, scoring 630 runs and taking 25 wickets. At Eastbourne in August, he hit 205 against Sussex. 'He occupied three hours over 100, but drove and pulled so well that he completed 200 in another eighty minutes and he hit a 5 and twenty-six 4's.' His own version of that innings is that, having completed a hundred, he was congratulated by 'Billy' Griffith, the Sussex wicket-keeper, who asked him if he had ever made a double century. When Bailey said that he had not Griffith suggested that he got his head down and went on for one. Such was the camaraderie of county cricket.

He had bowled and batted well in the Varsity match, performed creditably for the Gentlemen against the Players and it was apparent that here was an all-rounder of the highest quality of whom England had great need. There was joy and endeavour in his play. He would drop on one knee and pull the ball over square-leg, and he would race to the wicket when bowling, fingers of the left hand splayed at the moment of delivery. His fielding was outstanding, and he appeared to be capable of catching anything. He would be the man to confront Bradman's Australians in 1948. But it was not to be.

His all-round abilities were not restricted to cricket. He had become a highly competitive and dynamic soccer player. He won his blue in 1947 and 1948, and he was to play with distinction for Walthamstow Avenue and Leytonstone. He was also associated with Southend United and while he was playing for their reserves in the winter of 1947–48 he suffered an ankle injury which was to handicap him in the following cricket season. Far from being the triumphant confrontation with Australians for which one had hoped, the 1948 season was one of bitter disappointment. Edrich, a tremendous trier but hardly a bowler of enough pace or ability, Watkins, of whom the same could be said, Coxon and Pollard all shared the new ball with Bedser in the Test series, which is indicative of the state of English fast bowling at the time. Bailey, of whom much had been expected, had a season that was considered disappointing by his standards, 700 runs and 63 wickets. The figures were still better than some of those who had played for England that summer.

With his usual sense of fun, he considered that an injury sustained in the match between Essex and Bradman's Australians at Southend was fortuitous in that it enabled him to escape further punishment as his colleagues were beaten by an innings and 451 runs. Bailey retired after bowling 21 overs and taking 2 for 128. He has always boasted that Essex were the only side to bowl the Australians out in a day in 1948. Bradman's great side had a profound effect upon him, as Bailey himself revealed in *Wickets, Catches and a Few Odd Runs*.

'Although we bowled them out in one day, they did manage to amass the little matter of 721 runs. In the first half hour, fielding at backward slip, I made the elementary error of trying to catch a Sid Barnes hook, which broke a finger in my left hand. My fingers have always been too small and delicate for serious cricket and this break was only one of many, all done when fielding.

'There were several features about that Southend massacre. First, the Australians never accelerated – they kept plodding along at just under 250 runs per session. Second, I bowled Keith Miller first ball for nought with an absolutely straight ball. I remarked to Don that Keith had not appeared interested, to which he replied with the cryptic, "He'll learn". Third, although the attendance of 32,000 for the two days was easily a ground record, I have met subsequently at least one million people who claim to have been present. Finally, we managed somehow to bowl 129 overs, which was remarkable in six hours play considering the amount of time spent retrieving the ball from the boundary.

'In retrospect my lack of success, injuries and the arrival of the Australians in 1948 were good for me because until then I had not thought sufficiently about my game, nor worked enough at it. There were no genuinely fast bowlers in England and until 1948, as one of the fastest around, I still cherished the hope that I would become a bowler of real pace who would be able to blast out the opposition. The arrival of Ray Lindwall and Keith Miller changed all that, as their pace was yards faster; while the third member of what was essentially a three-pronged attack, Bill Johnston, was not only a much better bowler than myself, but also quicker.'

Trevor Bailey has ever been a thinking man, and what he had learned from the Australians was a professional application to ally to his amateur panache. In every respect, 1948 was the turning point of his career. The Australians were 'so far removed from the Cambridge and Essex players I knew'.

He could not have wished for a better start to the following season. The opening day of the season at Lord's saw him have Nigel Howard caught behind with the first delivery. He also made 82. The most significant match for him, however, was when he played for M.C.C. against the New Zealand tourists at Lord's in May. The New Zealanders were a very strong side, and their performances in the Tests, all four of which were restricted to three days and all four of which were drawn, brought about an alteration in the duration of Test matches thereafter. M.C.C. made 379 and on the Monday, Bailey, bowling at a considerable pace and very accurately, reduced the tourists to 96 for 6. He took four of the wickets, Sutcliffe, Walter Hadlee, Donnelly and Reid, and took a brilliant catch at forward short-leg to dismiss Wallace. Wallace hit the ball very hard, but Bailey, dropping on one knee, held the ball right-handed above his head. The catch framed an image which has remained in the memory. He finished with 5 for 83, and his selection for the first Test match was axiomatic.

He had an outstanding debut and a splendid first series. The New Zealanders were troubled by his pace and lift, and he had Scott caught at fourth slip with his eighth ball in Test cricket. Next ball Edrich dropped

Trevor Bailey. 'Ever a thinking man, he allied professional application to his amateur panache.'

Walter Hadlee at first slip, but in a post-lunch spell Bailey accounted for Hadlee and Wallace so that with New Zealand on 80 for 4, he had taken 3 for 31. He finished with 6 for 118.

In the second Test match, at Lord's, he scored 93, sharing a record sixth wicket stand of 189 with Denis Compton. The record was to be surpassed fourteen years later by Peter Parfitt and Barry Knight, Bailey's protégé.

It is worth noting what *Wisden* wrote of Bailey's batting in that Test: 'The change in England's fortunes came when Bailey joined Compton. Fortunate to receive two loose balls down the leg side which he turned for four apiece immediately he went in, Bailey showed complete confidence and for a long time he overshadowed Compton. Bailey continued to punish anything loose, mainly by going down on one knee and sweeping the ball hard to the square-leg boundary. Ten 4's came in his first 50 made in sixty-seven minutes . . . Bailey was unlucky to miss his first Test hundred, for with only seven wanted he cut a ball onto the wicket-keeper's foot, whence it rebounded into the hands of second slip. His splendid innings lasted two and a half hours and contained sixteen 4's.'

Trevor Bailey's batting and bowling was shaped to the needs of his side. He was not concerned with personal glory, only with winning or not being beaten.

In the third Test, he took 6 for 84 on a batsman's wicket and provided fast bowling that was full of venom. Then he hit 72 not out and shared a thrilling partnership of 105 with Reg Simpson. By the end of his first series, he had scored 219 runs, average 73, and taken 16 wickets, which was six more than any other England bowler.

His county season was equally successful. He completed the first of his eight 'doubles' on 1 August, and three weeks later, at Clacton, took all ten Lancashire wickets for 90. In this match, incidentally, Essex still lost by ten wickets inside two days. He was named as one of *Wisden*'s five cricketers of the year. 'Bailey runs up in smooth, straight manner for about nineteen paces and with a leap delivers the ball which comes quickly to the batsman. Bailey is always experimenting. He has already changed his action five times and is ready to do so again for the sake of improvement.' In view of what was to come, the assessment of his batting is significant. 'He would be quite content to play sound, steady cricket, but circumstances have tended to make him an aggressive player. He is an attractive stroke player with a fondness for the cut, but he can score freely with the drive and leg-side strokes.'

England had found her all-rounder, and a quick bowler.

He had been unable to accept the M.C.C.'s invitation to tour the West

Indies, 1947–48, but he now looked forward to a time of tours and Tests. The West Indies were the opposition in 1950, and England won the first Test with ease after an unhappy start. They were 88 for 5 before Evans and Bailey came together in a stand of 161, a record at the time. In contrast to the aggression of the previous season, he concentrated mainly on defence, and 'England were indebted to Bailey, who presented a straight bat in defence for over three and a half hours and occasionally opened his shoulders for the sweep or cut'. He scored 82 not out, but thereafter came disappointment as, troubled by strains and injuries, he was unable to play for England again until the fourth and last Test.

He was in the England party that went to Australia under Freddie Brown, 1950–51, although his selection was not welcomed by everyone, for some harboured doubts as to his stamina and consistency. He swept aside his critics with some fine bowling. At Brisbane, he took 3 for 28 on a perfect wicket as Australia were bowled out for 228. Then it rained, and thereafter batsmen were in constant bewilderment. He took 4 for 22 in the second innings, but England lost. There was more great bowling at Melbourne, 4 for 40 and 2 for 47, but again England lost. He had his thumb broken by a ball from Lindwall in the third Test, could not bowl nor play in the fourth Test, but he finished top of the England bowling averages. His batting form had deserted him in the Tests in Australia, but he hit 134 not out when England drew with New Zealand in Christchurch. It was to be his only Test century, yet he scored 2,290 runs in Test cricket and reached fifty ten times.

In Australia, Bailey bowled most intelligently. He knew the weaknesses of the opposing batsmen and probed at them, and he was always economical. The following summer, against the South Africans, he lost his way. His run-up faltered, and he failed to take a wicket in either of the Tests in which he played. At Headingley, he hit 95, but strained his back and had to retire from the attack. He did not play for England again until 1953.

This was a great year for English cricket, and it was to be a significant one for Trevor Bailey. In his absence from Test cricket, England had found a new fast bowler, Freddie Trueman, but Trueman was not in the side for the first four Tests against Australia, Bailey sharing the new ball with Alec Bedser. Bedser had a marvellous series. The first four Tests were drawn, but England, under Len Hutton, won the fifth and so regained the 'Ashes' which they had last won in 1932–33. It was a cause for much celebration. To regard the figures now at a cold distance is to miss the drama, character and fascination of the situation which grew more exciting as the series progressed. Bailey scored 222 runs, average

31·71, and took 8 wickets at 48·37 runs each. In themselves, these statistics may seem unremarkable, yet in that season and that series Trevor Bailey established himself unmistakably as one of the great personalities of English cricket, and he became a national hero. From that year onwards he was known as 'Barnacle' Bailey, and everything that he did in those five Test matches against Australia had meaning and moment.

In the first Test, at Trent Bridge, Australia had seemingly asserted their authority on the series. They were 237 for 3, but Bedser and Bailey took the new ball and they were all out for 249. In the second Test, at Lord's, Bailey failed to take a wicket, but he played one of the most memorable innings in Test cricket.

England led by 26 on the first innings, but Australia made 368 in their second knock so that the task facing the home side was a formidable one. It became more formidable when Hutton, Kenyon and Graveney were out for 12 runs. England's position could have been worse, for shortly before the close of the fourth day Willie Watson, the Yorkshire left-hander, was dropped at short-leg off Ring. Nevertheless, England began the last day with defeat looming. It became a near certainty when Denis Compton was leg before to Johnston at 12.40 p.m. Bailey joined Watson. What was now witnessed was one of the classic rearguard actions of Test cricket.

When Bailey, the last of the recognised batsmen, joined Watson nearly five hours remained for play. At first, the Australians, and Hassett their captain, did not appear unduly worried, believing that victory was an inevitability, 'but as Bailey settled down to his sternest defence, the bowlers produced all they knew. Still Bailey went on playing a dead-bat pendulum stroke to every ball on his wicket. His batting was far from attractive to the eye, but it was thoroughly efficient and founded in first principles.'

They survived safely until lunch and well into the afternoon. 'The most testing period came midway through the afternoon when Lindwall and Miller took the new ball. Both bowlers tried every trick and wile in their armoury, but they could not get through. Three times Bailey was struck on the hand by a bouncer, but after each he paused only to wring his hand. Then the struggle was joined anew.'

The stand was broken when Watson, having completed a noble century, fell to Ring. The partnership with Bailey had realised 163, and, more importantly, it had lasted until only 40 minutes of the match remained. Trevor Bailey was out shortly after Watson, much to his own annoyance. He had imposed the shackles of restraint upon himself because that was what his side needed of him. The first time he lost concentration he was out. He attempted a loose cover drive and was caught. He had batted for 257 minutes, scored 71, and England were safe.

The third Test was ruined by rain, but the fourth Test again moved in favour of Australia and again it was Bailey who came to England's rescue. England trailed by 99 on the first innings, and a mid-order collapse saw them at 182 for 6 in their second innings, and Compton retired hurt with an injured hand. Laker batted with exciting defiance and scored 48 out of a stand of 57 with Bailey. The Essex man now showed a passivity which surpassed his effort at Lord's. Time was a matter of urgency for both sides, and Bailey was intent on devouring it. He batted for 262 minutes and scored 38. His defiance meant that Australia were left with only 115 minutes in which to score 177 to win.

Hutton decided to rest Bailey as he had been on the field all day and to open the bowling with Bedser and Lock. From the start the Australians attacked the bowling. Lock was savaged for six an over. Laker's two overs produced 17 runs. When the third wicket fell and Davidson joined Hole only 66 were needed in 45 minutes.

Bailey now took command. He joined Bedser in the attack and bowled on and outside the leg stump. He blunted the Australian challenge. Hole was splendidly caught high above his head by Graveney on the square-leg boundary, and Australia finished on 147 for 4. Bailey had bowled six overs and taken 1 for 9. Once again England had been saved.

For the deciding Test match, England brought in Trueman to open the bowling with Bedser, Bailey becoming the third seamer in the side, a position that he was to fill with credit for the rest of his Test career. Australia were bowled out for 275. On the Monday, England disappointed. Compton was uncertain and the middle-order fell away, seven wickets falling for 100 runs.

'Bailey had begun with 15 in thirty-five minutes, but on being joined by Laker he changed his methods and brilliant strokes to the off gave him 11 in an over from Johnston. Laker soon went, but Lock closed an end for the last forty minutes of a dramatic day, England finishing at 235 for seven wickets – Bailey 35, Lock 4.'

Lock went without addition on the Tuesday, but first with Trueman and then with Bedser, with whom 44 were added for the last wicket, Bailey steered England to a invaluable and unexpected first innings lead of 31. Next day England regained the 'Ashes'.

No man had contributed more in the series than Trevor Bailey. He never coveted easy runs, nor cheap wickets. He was always at his best when he was most needed and where the fight was thickest.

Hutton took the England side to the West Indies a few months after the victory over Australia. West Indies won the first two Tests, the third went to England and the fourth was drawn. The deciding Test was played at Sabina Park, Kingston, Jamaica, where West Indies had never been beaten. Hutton lost the toss for the fourth time in the series, and with Statham unfit, Bailey, the vice-captain for the tour, opened the bowling with Trueman. His fifth ball had Holt brilliantly caught at short-leg by Lock. Forty minutes later West Indies were in total disarray on a perfect batting pitch, four men were out for 13, three wickets had fallen to Trevor Bailey. He cut a ball back sharply off the seam to bowl Weekes, had Stollmeyer caught behind and ended resistance by Atkinson. On a wicket on which West Indies had relished the opportunity to bat first, Bailey finished with 7 for 34, and England faced a first innings total of only 139.

Bailey then went out to open the England batting with Len Hutton. They played out safely until the close and with greatest caution until after lunch on the second day, by which time the turf had eased, having recovered from its sweating under the covers overnight. The stand brought 43 runs. Bailey made 23. Hutton went on to score a double century, and England levelled the series. Bailey was caught behind off a young all-rounder named Gary Sobers who was making his Test debut.

When Hutton was out of the England side in 1954 it was David Sheppard who was called upon to captain the side. Bailey opened the batting with the new skipper at Old Trafford and scored 42, but he was never asked to captain England. Strangely, some years later, a computer, having been fed all the relevant data, chose Bailey as the ideal England captain of a very strong side.

England now faced the supreme test as Hutton took the side to Australia in defence of the 'Ashes'. In the first Test, at Brisbane, he won the toss and asked Australia to bat. Australia made 601 for 8 declared, Bailey 3 for 140. England were bowled out for 190 and 257. Bailey, batting with a hand strapped because of injury, scored 88 and 23.

The second Test, at Sydney, was the one in which Frank Tyson leashed his fury upon the old enemy, and his 6 for 85 in the second innings has tended to obliterate important events earlier in that match which England won by 38 runs. Injuries again made it necessary that Bailey be pressed into service as an opener. He failed, with 0 and 6. England were bowled out for 154 in the first innings, and Australia looked set for a big lead. Bailey had Arthur Morris taken at leg slip before the close of the first day, and next morning he accounted for Favell and Burke. The Australian lead was restricted to 74, and Bailey had 4 for 59. Valuable runs and wickets continued to come his way in the rest of that triumphant series. An England side without Bailey was unthinkable. He had become a national institution. He had also become recognised as one of the most chivalrous as well as one of the toughest of opponents. In the last Test of the 1954–55 series, he hit out at everything as England moved towards a declaration. It was the last over before tea when Hutton would have closed the innings and Lindwall was bowling what everyone believed, mistakenly, would be his last over against England in Test cricket. Bailey, on 72, allowed himself to be bowled, so giving the great fast bowler, for whom he had so much admiration, his hundredth wicket in Tests against England.

Lindwall, in fact, was back in England in 1956. This was the series which Laker dominated and England won 2–1. Bailey missed the last Test through injury, but he was, as ever, part of the triumph.

Peter May had taken over from Hutton as England's captain, and Doug Insole, Bailey's close friend, was named as vice-captain for the trip to South Africa. May had a poor series, and Colin Cowdrey stated his unwillingness to open the innings. Bailey was forced into the role and became more than an adequate stop-gap. He hit 80 in the third Test at Durban and shared an opening stand of 115 with Peter Richardson. In the second innings he had his right hand fractured by a short ball from Heine, but he resumed his innings with his hand in plaster and scored three more runs in 55 minutes before being caught off Tayfield. This brave effort did much to help England save the match and eventually draw the series. In the next Test, at Johannesburg, he had match figures of 5 for 66 and scored 13 and 1. It was his forty-seventh Test, and he had completed the 'double'.

In the Test match averages, Insole, Richardson and Cowdrey finished above him in the batting, and he headed the bowling with 19 wickets at 12·21 runs each.

The West Indies, first frustrated by May and Cowdrey at Edgbaston, were well beaten at Lord's, Headingley and The Oval in 1957. At Lord's, they were routed in three days. Bailey took 7 for 44 in the first innings and finished the game on the Saturday afternoon when he took 4 for 54. His eleven wickets in the match equalled the England record against the West Indies. It was his fiftieth Test.

A golden age of English Test cricket was drawing to a close, however. In the autumn of 1958, Peter May set out for Australia at the head of what looked on paper to be a very strong England side, but in a rather miserable series they were outplayed and lost 4–0, with one match drawn and that only because Australia scorned the opportunity to attempt to score 150 in 100 minutes to win.

The first Test set a depressing pattern for the series. England made 134 and 198. Australia scored 186 and 147 for 2. In England's second innings, on a slow wicket, Bailey batted for 357 minutes to reach his fifty, and his innings of 68 took 458 minutes. His was the slowest fifty in first-class cricket. On the last day Burke hit 28 in 250 minutes. There was less justification for these displays than there had been at Lord's five years earlier.

Trevor Bailey was again needed as an opening batsman for the remaining four Tests. Cowdrey registered the slowest hundred in Tests between the two countries, later beaten by Woolmer, and there was tedium and concern about bowling actions.

At Melbourne, from 13 to 18 February, Bailey played his last Test match. He was twice dismissed by Ray Lindwall, the bowler to whom he had sacrificed his wicket four years earlier, without scoring, and he failed to take a wicket.

He had played 61 Test matches, and he is one of only four English Test players to have scored more than two thousand runs and taken over a hundred wickets in Test cricket.

He played first-class cricket for another eight years. He was secretary and captain of Essex, and he encouraged Barry Knight to succeed him as England's leading all-rounder. He scored well over twenty thousand runs and took more than two thousand first-class wickets, but he can never be measured in figures, impressive as they are.

He was the most thoughtful and analytical of cricketers, and he has brought these qualities to refresh the commentary box. He wanted to win and he hated to lose, and he has refreshed the commentary box with these qualities too, for his broadcasting, like his writing, has a sense of passionate commitment. He groomed and encouraged many of the Essex players who were to bring the county glory in later years, and he taught them to play hard and enjoy it.

Whether he was bowling quickly, fielding brilliantly, batting briskly or defending doggedly, Trevor Bailey was always doing it with zest and love, and none who loves the game could fail to recognise that. He touched all with intelligence and no other all-rounder in the England team since the end of the Second World War, save Botham, could so influence the course of a match.

7

MILLER AND HIS DISCIPLE

Australia has always been strongest when she could call on a great all-rounder. Giffen, Noble and Armstrong were all at their height when Australia was strongest, and Bradman's powerful side of the years immediately after the Second World War was rich in all-round strength. As Bailey was making his mark in matches at Lord's in the closing years of the war a young Australian arrived on the scene to thrill all with his exhilarating batting and dynamic fast bowling. Keith Miller is one of the very few cricketers in the history of the game who would have been picked for any country as a batsman or as a bowler. It was truly said of him by Reg Hayter, 'Nearly every captain of a country defeated by Australia in her magnificent post-war run believed that, with Miller on his side, the issue would have been far closer, or have gone the other way.'

The strange things about Miller are that, although he grew to be 6 feet, 2 inches tall and to weigh 13½ stone, he was small enough as a boy to cherish hopes that he would become a jockey, and that he was not considered as a bowler until he began to fire down a few overs for the Australian Services in England at the end of the war.

He was born in Melbourne in 1919, in the month of the Melbourne Cup, appropriate for one who was to carry a passion for the turf. He was christened Keith Ross after Keith and Ross Smith who were near the end of their historic flight from England to Australia in November 1919. He moved through grade cricket in Melbourne, and he was greatly influenced by Hugh Carroll of South Melbourne who, it is argued, is the only coach from whom Miller ever accepted advice. Carroll's philosophy was to hit the ball hard and high.

In 1939–40, he was in the Victoria side in the Sheffield Shield. His fourth match was against South Australia at Melbourne, and he hit 108. The veteran leg-spinner Clarrie Grimmett was in the visitors' side and he suggested to the young Miller that he should take up bowling as it was a more satisfying art form than batting. A challenge was always something that appealed to Miller. He mused on Grimmett's advice, but he went off to the war, not before he had played a few non-Sheffield Shield games in 1940–41, met Grimmett again and bowled seven overs in first-class cricket in one of which he had captured the wicket of Ridings.

He served in the RAAF. He flew Mosquitoes and earned a reputation as a dashing, devil-may-care night-fighter pilot. There has always been something essentially romantic about him, his looks, his love of the good life and serious music, his adoration of racing and his courtesy. He has been one of those for whom every minute slept has been a minute wasted.

Stationed in England, he played cricket for the Australian Services. He was totally unknown in England at the time, but he quickly became the most exciting player to come out of the war. He made a deep impression when playing for the RAAF against Sir Pelham Warner's XI at the beginning of June 1943. Warner's XI got 201, Miller taking 2 for 20 as the seventh bowler used. He then hit 45 out of 100. The RAAF did not show up well, but 'in Miller they possessed a batsman of ability, graceful drives and crisp cuts bringing him 45 out of 53 in just over half an hour'. Later in the season, also at Lord's, he hit 91 and took 3 for 23 against the RAF. He should have done the hat trick, but a catch was dropped.

In 1944, Lord's buzzed with excitement every time he came to the wicket. On August Bank Holiday Monday, 'England' made 226 and 'Australia' were left 3¼ hours in which to get the runs. They failed, but Miller hit 85 out of 119 in 100 minutes and sent a thrill through the 16,000 spectators.

The 'Victory' Tests provided him with the stage most suited to his personality and taste. There was joy in the air. He topped the Australian batting averages, hit two centuries and began to bowl more. He was very fast and very wild. Stumps went flying, but on occasions the ball went hurtling down the leg side for four wides.

The most memorable match in that summer of 1945 came on 25, 27 and 28 August when England met the Dominions. Cricket at Lord's was entertaining and exciting throughout the war. There were one-day matches, studded with famous names and played in a festival spirit, but there was a sense of unreality about it all. The 1945 season offered something different, for a few three-day first-class matches were played, still studded with stars and still played in a festival spirit. The England–Dominions match was played before packed houses, produced 1,241 runs and saw the Dominions win by 45 runs with eight minutes to spare. Naïvely, some of us believed it would always be like this. The best period of a very fine match came on the last day.

'The final stage will be remembered chiefly for the glorious driving of Miller. He outshone everyone by his dazzling hitting. In ninety minutes he raised his overnight 61 to 185, and in three-quarters of an hour of superb cricket he and Constantine put on 117. Though travelling at such a pace, Miller played faultlessly. One of his seven 6's set the whole crowd talking. It was a terrific on-drive off Hollies, and the ball lodged in the small roof of the broadcasting box above the England players' dressing-room. Besides his 6's Miller hit thirteen 4's, his 185 taking him only two and three-quarter hours. This was a wonderful finish to the season at Lord's where in four first-class matches he scored 568 runs in eight innings, twice not out, with three centuries and an average of 94·68.'

It was apparent that Miller possessed the right temperament for the important occasion, indeed he revelled in it, and that he possessed the ability to shape his innings according to the state of the game. Pressed into service more as a bowler after Cheetham had returned to Australia, he emerged as the liveliest bowler to be seen in England, wild, but very fast.

More importantly, perhaps, Miller had revealed a gift not given to many; he demanded a reaction from the spectator. When Miller was playing, you were part of the game. He settled at the crease, gave a toss of the head which shook his mane of hair back into place, stroked his thigh pad into position and exuded a sense of power. When he raced in to bowl he excited a response. Either you urged him on or your heart beat in anger and apprehension at what he might do to the batsman. His bowling was destined to be restricted by a back injury he received when he skilfully crash-landed his stricken aircraft in Norfolk, but it was always to be quick enough and menacing enough.

The first post-war season in Australia saw the emergence of several good players, although there was no Sheffield Shield competition. Foremost among them was Ray Lindwall, a 24 year old fast bowler from New South Wales, who had spent three years of the war in the jungles of New Guinea and the Solomon Islands. He could also bat a bit and took a century off the Queensland bowlers in Sydney. In New South Wales's next match, he took 3 for 55 and 3 for 40 against the Australian Services. He was confonted by Keith Miller for the first time, and Miller hit 105 not out in the first innings. In the next few years the names of Lindwall and Miller were to become inseparably linked. They were two of seven Australians who made their Test match debuts in the first Test to be played after the war, New Zealand v Australia, at Wellington, March 1946. For some strange reason the match was not recognised as a Test match until two years later, but it marked the beginning of the Miller–Lindwall association.

New Zealand unwisely chose to bat first on a rain-affected pitch and were bowled out for 42 by Toshack and O'Reilly, who was playing his last Test. Australia, led by Bill Brown, made 199 for 8 declared. Brown made 67, Barnes 54 and Miller 30. In the second innings, Miller opened the bowling with Lindwall for the first time. He sent back Hadlee and Scott at a personal cost of 6 runs in six overs, and New Zealand were bowled out for 54.

In 1946–47, Victoria swept all before them in the first Sheffield Shield competition for seven years. They beat South Australia by nine wickets, Miller hitting 188 with one of the finest batting displays ever seen in Adelaide. He missed the victory over Queensland, but hit 153 against New South Wales, including Lindwall and Toshack, who were beaten by an innings. He made only 81 in the second match against Queensland, in Brisbane, but hit 206 not out against New South Wales in Sydney. His 667 runs for Victoria were scored at an average of 133·40. He bowled only 65·4 overs, but took 10 for 231. In that same Australian season, England felt his full blast for the first time.

He did nothing with the bat and bowled only four overs in his first meetings with the M.C.C. team, for Victoria and for an Australian XI, but the first Test match brought him back to hurricane force. Hammond's side was ill-prepared to meet such opposition as they encountered in Australia and had the worst record of any England touring side. At Brisbane, where Australia had never previously won, the home side recovered from 46 for 2 with a stand of 276 by Bradman and Hassett. Miller then came in and hit 79, sharing a stand of 106 with Hassett. During this partnership the two Victorians savaged the England attack to such an extent that the fielding disintegrated. From that point any hope that England had in the series was gone. The tourists batted twice after violent storms. They were out for 141 and 172. In fact, the pitch played better than expected, and Lindwall retired from the Australian attack with chicken-pox, but Miller was devastating, rearing the ball at batsmen from a length and taking 7 for 60 in the first innings and 2 for 17 in the second.

Australia won three Tests and two were drawn. Lindwall hit 100 in 113 minutes in the third Test, and Miller hit the first of his seven Test hundreds in the fourth Test, at Adelaide. He and Lindwall bounced the ball freely, and the majority of the England batsmen were totally unable to cope.

Miller had a high and perfect action, and he was capable of making a

Keith Miller goes to the wicket in the company of Doug Ring. 'Nearly every captain of a country defeated by Australia in her magnificent post-war run believed that, with Miller on his side, the issue would have been far closer, or have gone the other way.'

ball rise steeply from just short of a good length. He considered it a good weapon against batsmen who were indifferent hookers, but who instinctively essayed a hook at a bouncer. It was, too, a delivery which initially he bowled in response to calls from the crowd, and later because it drew a response.

At the end of his first series against England he was second to Bradman in the batting averages, and second to Lindwall in the bowling. Lindwall's 18 wickets had cost 20·38 runs apiece; Miller's had cost 20·87. In one series they had established a fast bowling partnership that was spoken of in the same breath as Gregory and McDonald or Larwood and Voce.

They drew closer together in 1947–48 when Keith Miller moved to New South Wales. In this season, Australia overwhelmed India. Miller hit two bright fifties, and on one occasion reduced India to 6 for 2, but, like Trevor Bailey, he was never interested in cheap runs or wickets. Australia were so superior to India in this series that they did not need his talents, and he drifted through the Tests with an air of indifference.

We have mentioned how he was bowled for 0 on the day that the Australians piled up the runs against Essex at Southchurch Park. He wanted a challenge. It was the excitement of positive confrontation that brought the best out of him. The first Test between England and Australia to be played in England since the war was such an occasion. Only twenty minutes' play was possible before lunch on the first day at Trent Bridge, but during that time Miller set his mark on the match by bowling Len Hutton, England's great hope, for 3 with an extra fast delivery. He finished with 3 for 38, and, with Lindwall unable to bowl in the second innings because of a groin strain, he sent down 44 overs and took 4 for 125 as England struggled valiantly to recover. He dismissed both openers, Hutton and Washbrook, and later accounted for Denis Compton who played one of his greatest innings. He got Compton with a bouncer. It was not an unexpected delivery, but as Compton moved on to the back foot and prepared to hook the ball was on him. It was quicker than he had expected and he tumbled on his wicket.

Miller was troubled with his back throughout that tour, and his batting was rarely needed in the Tests, even at number five, but he again finished second to Lindwall in the bowling and passed a thousand runs for the tour.

By now, he was regarded with suspicion by some of those in authority. He showed no sign of trying to hide his feelings when the occasion lacked seriousness or competitiveness, nor did he conceal his love of racing, symphony concerts and the night-life. He was noted as a rebel, and to the astonishment of followers of the game in England, he was omitted from the Australian side to tour South Africa in 1949–50. Fate played a hand, however. Johnston was injured in a car crash, and Miller was hurriedly flown to South Africa to bolster the party. He played in all five Tests and had an outstanding all-round series as Australia again triumphed.

Australia's run of twenty-five consecutive Tests without defeat (twenty of them won) came to an end in March 1951, but by then Australia had already taken a four–nil lead in the series. Miller, having hit 214 against M.C.C. for New South Wales, topped the Australian batting averages in the series and was second in the bowling to the mystery spinner Iverson.

Later the same year, he accepted the challenge of the West Indian spinners, Ramadhin and Valentine, who had destroyed England, and finished second in both batting and bowling averages. He hit 129 in the second Test at Sydney where he and Hassett put on 235 for the fourth wicket, which remains an Australian record against West Indies. Whether batting, bowling or fielding (he was one of the very best of slip fielders), there was an infectious enthusiasm about Miller's cricket.

In 1952–53, Australia failed to win a Test series for the first time since the war when Jack Cheetham's South Africans surprised all by levelling the rubber with a win in the last Test from which both Lindwall and Miller were absent through injury. Miller still ended top of the bowling averages.

On slower wickets in England in 1953 he had a less happy time, but he hit a fine century at Lord's which gave Australia the scent of victory that was to be denied by Watson and Bailey, and at Headingley he took 4 for 63 to break through the England batting in the second innings and again give Australia hope of a victory which was thwarted by Bailey's leg theory.

The wheel had now turned, but when Hutton's men unleashed Tyson and Statham on Australia in 1954–55 Miller was still able to hinder the progress of England on occasions. At Melbourne, with the series levelled at one Test each, he opened the bowling on a wicket which offered only very little help to the bowler and sent back Hutton, Edrich and Compton to send the visitors tumbling to 41 for 4.

There were many who believed that this would be his last series, but he was off to the West Indies immediately after the defeat by England. He hit 147 in the first Test and led Australia in the field after Ian Johnson had injured a hand while batting. Australia won by 9 wickets. He hit centuries in the fourth and fifth Tests, and in the fifth Test he also took 8 wickets. He finished second to Neil Harvey in the batting averages and took 20 wickets in the five Tests to play a most significant part in Australia's victory.

He had captained New South Wales with distinction, but after their Sheffield Shield win in 1956, a season in which he was much troubled by injury, he decided to retire. First, he was to make his final tour to England. It was the summer of Laker's triumph, and, arguably, the poorest showing ever by an Australian side in England, but Miller was fourth in the Australian batting and, with 21 wickets, topped the bowling and took more wickets in the series than any other bowler bar Laker himself. He won Australia their one Test victory with match figures of 10 for 152 at Lord's, and had he been fit to bowl at Headingley the series might have had a different ending.

He played the last of his fifty-five Tests a month after the end of the tour of England when, on a matting wicket in Karachi, Pakistan beat Australia for the first time. He was top scorer in the first innings, 21 out of 80. In the second, he scored 11. He took 2 wickets in the match which, ironically, was the Test in which his partner Ray Lindwall reached 200 wickets.

It was not quite the end of his cricket. In 1959, he was made an honorary member of M.C.C. He was touched by the honour and wished to make a gesture to the Club so asked if he could play for them against Oxford University. To warm up for this game he turned out for Nottinghamshire, who were having a hard time, against Cambridge University. He took 2 for 35, and made 62 and 102. He was 40 years old, and in the following week, for M.C.C. against Oxford, he was forced to call it a day because of injury.

He was a cricketer who could turn a game by a shot, an over or a catch. He excited crowds, for he could reshape a match, and do it with fun. He was aggressive, but almost casual, and although he was proud of his achievements, records and averages meant nothing to him. Yet his record is formidable. He took 170 wickets and scored nearly three thousand runs in Test cricket, and only one other Australian has approached that record.

That he never captained Australia in a series is a travesty. The Australian Board have been wont to make some strange appointments over the years, and the selection of Ian Johnson ahead of Miller is still one that remains incomprehensible. It was a choice based on prejudice and not on the respective merits of the two cricketers, and Miller was hurt by it. 'Nugget' has a heart of gold, but it can extend to a sense of injustice.

He led New South Wales from 1953 to 1956, and under him the state began a run of nine successive Sheffield Shield titles. Stories about him, many of them apocryphal, abound. The most delightful is of an alleged incident when New South Wales were taking the field one day and one of the players said, 'Hey, Nugget, we have twelve players on the field.' Without turning his head, the skipper is supposed to have said, 'One of you bugger off and the rest scatter.'

It is a story that does justice to the imp in the man, but not to his quality as a captain. 'The very best captain I ever played under was Keith Miller,' asserts Richie Benaud. 'He was a magnificent cricketer and a great captain. No one under whom I played sized up a situation more quickly and no one was better at summing up a batsman's weaknesses. He had to do this for himself when he was bowling and it was second nature for him to do so as a captain.'

Keith Miller wanted to win, and he never wanted the game, or life, to be predictable or dull. He was a cricketer 'who could have played in any era and been an eye-catching favourite with everyone who followed the game. He taught me many things either by word or by example.'

The speaker is Richie Benaud, considered by many to be the finest of Australian captains and the only Australian to have an all-round record in Test cricket comparable to that of Keith Miller. The distinction between them should be made immediately. Miller would have played for any country as a batsman or as a bowler. He was a brilliant fielder. Benaud was a brilliant fielder and a leg-break bowler of the very highest quality. He should have walked into a Test side for his bowling, but because he was a leg-spinner in an age when the art was dying it was necessary for him to develop his talents as a batsman. He does not think he would have survived at international level if he had not done so, and here is the bowler who has taken more wickets in Test cricket than any other Australian save Lillee.

He learned his cricket from his father, a school-teacher and grade cricketer who bowled leg-breaks with great success. In 1948–49, he played one game for New South Wales as a batsman and scored 2. The following season, he played an innings of 93 against South Australia and took 5 wickets in the Sheffield Shield. By 1950–51, he was established, but his opportunities to bowl were still limited. A year later, he was in the Australian side for the fifth Test against West Indies at Sydney.

There was no immediate success for Benaud although he did take 4 for 118 against South Africa at Adelaide in the drawn series, 1952–53. The Australians stuck to the principle of the leg-spinner longer than most, and both he and Ring played in that series and were in the party that came to

Tom Dollery, the Warwickshire captain, claps Australian captain Hassett and his partner Richie Benaud as they leave the field. Benaud went on to become one of the very greatest of Test captains. A leg-break bowler and attacking batsman, Benaud brought excitement and intelligence to all that he did on the cricket field.

England a few months later. Neither of them was a success, and most people felt that Benaud would not be seen in England again.

He took 4 for 120 against Hutton's side in the fourth Test in Melbourne, January 1955, but three of the wickets were tail-enders, and he did not have a successful series. There was a general feeling that he was a lucky cricketer and that few others had been given such an extended run for so little return.

The tide began to turn in the West Indies a few months later. In Georgetown he took 3 wickets in four balls, and at Kingston he hit 121, reaching his century in 78 minutes. His first fifty came in 38 minutes, and suddenly he was being talked about.

It was apparent that here was a positive cricketer in all that he did. In his bowling, still maturing, he attempted to put the batsman under constant pressure. In the field, he was electric while his batting, though orthodox, breathed aggression.

Nevertheless, his second tour of England, 1956, was only marginally more successful than his first. He hit Australia's highest score in the series, a whirlwind 97 out of 117 at Lord's, but his 8 wickets cost more than 40 runs each. It was Laker's series, and as we have said elsewhere this was one of the poorest Australian sides ever to visit England.

Miller ended his Test career on the way home to Australia who now had a greater need than ever for an all-rounder of international quality. Benaud's immediate response was to take 7 for 72 in Madras, where Australia beat India by an innings, and to return match figures of 11 for 105 in Calcutta, where Australia again triumphed.

Those Test matches in India had a significant influence on Benaud's future. The responsibility of being Australia's leading all-rounder now rested firmly upon his shoulders and he had tasted success. Responsibility and success were to be the guiding forces of the rest of his career. Allied to this facet of his character were the intelligence and resolve which were to make him one of the greatest of captains. He had worked hard at his batting to ensure himself a permanent place in first-class cricket, now the thought and work he had put into his bowling, tempered by experience, began to bear fruit.

He went to South Africa with Ian Craig's team in 1957–58 and dominated the tour. 'The outstanding personality was R. Benaud, who, in bowling and batting, enjoyed a tour of unbroken success. Adding the googly to his leg-break and top-spinner, Benaud once more revealed the South African's dislike of flighted spin, bowled out of the back of the hand.'

He took 106 wickets on the tour, two more than any other bowler on a tour of South Africa, and 30 of these wickets came in the Tests where four times he took 5 wickets in an innings. 'Only in the first Test did Benaud fail to cause chaos with the ball, but he scored 122 in that match. He also hit another century in the fourth Test. Benaud's aggressive batting made him a great favourite with the crowds and his all-round skill was a major factor in the Australian success.'

Ian Craig was six months short of his 23rd birthday when he captained Australia for the first time. His appointment as captain of New South Wales and then of Australia must have made Benaud, five years his senior, believe that he would never lead either state or country. Miller had been frustrated by the appointment of Ian Johnson as Australia's captain, but Benaud and Craig were on friendly terms and Benaud's performances in South Africa showed clearly that he was willing and able to play under the young man. At this time none thought of Benaud as captain of Australia, for Neil Harvey had been understudy to Craig and was senior to Benaud.

Debate ensued when, on his return from South Africa, Ian Craig became ill with hepatitis. Benaud was named as captain of New South Wales for the opening Sheffield Shield match. Neil Harvey was also in the side, having just transferred from Victoria. Craig returned for the second match of the season and took over the captaincy, but he failed to score. He also failed to score for New South Wales against Peter May's touring side, and, obviously still unfit, he withdrew from the Australian XI side to meet M.C.C. and from first-class cricket for the rest of the season. He was never to play Test cricket again.

Harvey replaced Craig as captain of the Australian XI which lost to M.C.C., but Benaud was elected as captain of Australia for the Test series and enjoyed a season of unending success. He led New South Wales to the Sheffield Shield title and with 82 wickets in the season, he equalled Grimmett's record for a leg-spinner in an Australian season. Thirty-one of his wickets came in the Test matches.

It cannot have been easy for the selectors to have chosen him as captain ahead of Harvey, a good and faithful servant, but the general opinion is that he was named because his play in South Africa, with bat and ball, was permeated by the aggression and positivity of which Australia, and cricket, was in much need.

The 1958–59 series was one that was punctuated by controversy and dullness. There was English anger at the bowling actions of Meckiff and Rorke among others, and there was tedium in the batting, only 106 runs on the fourth day of the first Test. For England, the tour was a bitter disappointment; for Benaud, it was a triumph. To him, *Wisden* ascribed the reason for success. 'Australia possessed an inspiring leader in Benaud. He set an example of keen and fearless fielding by often posting himself close to the bat and, except for the Third Test when, with Australia two victories to the good, he closed up the game with an exaggerated defensive field, his handling of the team did him credit. Moreover, his bowling prowess with the leg-break, top-spinner and googly made him one of Australia's best players.' Australia won by four Tests to nil so that his place in cricket history was assured.

A year later, he led Australia to magnificent series victories in both Pakistan and India. His own contribution, especially with the ball, was outstanding. He encouraged his side to play exciting, entertaining cricket, and they responded. He had emerged as a man capable of persuading his players to act as a team, and he drew from everyone performance and commitment. He responded to their efforts with enthusiasm, and there are those who would blame him for the introduction of hugging and back-slapping into cricket.

Whatever may be the truth of that matter, it is indisputable that Benaud had lifted Australian cricket from the doldrums at a time when the game itself needed a boost. The nine months between 9 December 1960 and 22 August 1961 brought his achievements to a memorable climax. Worrell's West Indians lost to Benaud's Australians in one of the most exciting Test series in cricket history. The first Test was tied, and the last Test was won by Australia by two wickets when the ninth wicket pair scampered a bye. A record 90,800 watched the second day of that last Test at Melbourne, and the West Indians, though vanquished, departed amid a heroes' parade.

At the outset of the tour Worrell had insisted that his side was intent on putting back some of the lost adventure into cricket which, internationally, had become a dull and lifeless pastime. Benaud was adamant in his support of this ideal. The two captains were greeted with scepticism, but by the end of the series they had proved their words. 'Summer's glorious pastime had returned as a spectacle of some consequence and faith in the game was restored among the all-important younger fraternity on whom its popularity, and indeed its very existence, depends. That Worrell and Benaud were the leaders cannot be stressed too much. Upon their insistence on attractive, sensible cricket was laid the foundations of a true demonstration of this great game.'

During the series Benaud took his two hundredth Test wicket, but he was already beginning to be troubled by a shoulder injury which restricted the amount he was able to spin the ball. It kept him out of the second Test match against England at Lord's, June 1961, which Australia won. England drew level at Headingley. The fourth Test match, at Old Trafford, was a memorable one and was the scene of Benaud's finest performance against England.

England led by 177 on the first innings, but Australia fought back bravely and, helped by a last wicket stand of 98 between Davidson and McKenzie, they reached 432 in their second innings. This left England 230 minutes in which to score 256, or in which to save the match.

The wicket was playing well. There was only the remote danger that the rough made by Trueman's footholds could be exploited by a bowler, but the worn patch was outside the right-handed batsman's leg stump.

Pullar and Subba Row began with a brisk partnership of 40, and after Pullar had fallen to Davidson, Ted Dexter came in to give a glorious display of controlled hitting which made victory for England seem almost certain. Benaud, bowling into the rough, subdued the left-handed Subba Row who, naturally, found life harder than the right-handers, but Dexter shredded the rest of the Australian attack. In 84 minutes he hit 76 which included a six and 14 fours. He and Subba Row added 110 in as many minutes, and then came a decisive change brought about by astute captaincy and intelligent bowling.

Benaud chose to go round the wicket and attempt to pitch his leg-breaks into the rough outside the leg stump. Attempting to square cut the last ball of Benaud's over, Dexter was caught behind. The different angle of flight meant that the ball was too close to Dexter's body for the shot and the batsman paid the price.

Even with Dexter gone, England needed only 106 in as many minutes with 8 wickets remaining so that they hardly looked likely to be facing defeat. Then came a dramatic delivery. Benaud pitched the ball in the rough well outside May's leg stump. The batsman attempted a sweep. The ball turned back sharply and bowled him round his legs. Close, in the course of ten balls from Benaud, courted disaster as many times before clouting the ball straight to backward square leg. Subba Row was bowled by the last ball before tea.

In 85 minutes after tea, England needed 93 to win with 5 wickets standing, but there was little hope of victory now, and soon it became apparent that defeat for England was the most probable outcome of the match. Murray and Allen were taken at slip off Benaud. Barrington was leg before to Mackay. Benaud himself caught Trueman off Simpson, and when Alan Davidson bowled Statham, Australia had won a remarkable victory by 54 runs with half an hour to spare. They had retained the 'Ashes'.

All of the Australian players congratulated their skipper as he led them from the field. England remained stunned, beaten by shock in a match in which they had led all the way. The sight of Benaud's undisguised delight when he bowled May round his legs will stay with those who saw it for a very long time. He could not contain his joy and practically shook hands with himself. On that last afternoon he had a spell of bowling which produced 5 for 12 in 25 balls and won the match. His final figures were 6 for 70.

He led Australia when they fought off the challenge of Dexter's side in 1962–63. New South Wales beat M.C.C. by an innings at the start of the tour, Benaud taking 3 for 61 and 7 for 18, and in the first Test he took 6 for 115, but he fell away a little as the season progressed.

In the next Australian season, Benaud led Australia in the first Test against South Africa. The match was drawn, but he took 5 for 68. He could not play in the second Test because of injury, and Simpson took over the captaincy. Benaud announced that he would be retiring at the end of the rubber, and when he came back for the third Test he played under Simpson. His last Test was at Sydney when he took 4 for 118. He had played in 63 Tests, scored 2,201 runs and taken 248 wickets, a feat unequalled by any other Australian. He had never lost a series in which he captained Australia, and, indeed, he had only tasted defeat four times in his twenty-eight Tests as the captain of his country, which is why many consider him to be the best of Australian captains.

Off the field he has done much for Australian cricket by his expertise in public relations. Courteous, highly intelligent, perceptive and witty, he was the ideal cricketing ambassador. He lost some popularity, and some friends, in Australia because of his association with the Packer Enterprise, but he retained his dignity and his strength of character. As a commentator and journalist, he is among the very best, and he is an unceasing worker, typing away furiously on a book or a project when he is not on the air.

The quietly effective wit of his comment gets to the heart of a situation. With Botham tearing into bowl at Edgbaston in 1981 and the crowd roaring, he assessed the atmosphere in one phrase – 'The score at the moment is Lions 1, Christians 0'. And when Dilley, having been baited by the crowd on one occasion, chose to give them the V-sign in return when he took a wicket Benaud's only comment was, 'I think you have to be a very good bowler before you do that.'

He learned from Miller, who was a greater player, and he was luckier than Miller in the opportunities offered to him and the breadth of the stage on which he was allowed to perform, but the game has been better for having Richie Benaud as part of it, and ultimately it was cricket that was lucky that he should have infused it with so much vibrancy.

8

WEST INDIAN KNIGHTS

The supremacy in international cricket which had been with Australia while Benaud was captain passed to West Indies on his retirement, and, with one or two stumbles, it has remained with them ever since. For the past decade the West Indian side has been composed almost exclusively of six batsmen, a wicket-keeper batsman and four very fast bowlers. There have been some alterations to this balance, notably in the inclusion of Roger Harper, an off-spin bowler, excellent batsman and fielder of the very highest quality, but in recent years West Indian cricket has been known for power rather than subtlety. However, the two greatest all-round cricketers to come from the islands combined both these qualities.

When England met the Dominions in 1945 in the match in which Keith Miller hit his magnificent 185 the Dominions side was captained by Learie Nicholas Constantine, fast bowler, marvellous hitter and fielder supreme, the best all-rounder that the West Indies produced before the arrival of Gary Sobers. That he was captain in that match was the greatest tribute to the man himself. Lindsay Hassett was due to captain the side but he had fallen ill, and on the eve of the match the players, nine Australians and a New Zealander, chose Constantine as their skipper. Even in the late stages of the war it was not customary for a black man to captain a side that had white men in it, and the West Indies themselves were to rely on 'white' captains until Worrell changed all. The honour that was given to Constantine in August 1945 was a tribute from young men who admired him as a cricketer and who respected him greatly as a man, as did all who met him. He responded by leading his side to a thrilling victory, his own memorable contribution being an innings of 40 in the 45-minute stand with Keith Miller. He was then 43 years old, and his first-class career and Test career, limited by today's standards, were behind him.

He played only 18 Test matches, scored 635 runs and took 58 wickets. He also made 28 catches and C.L.R. James suggested that he was the only all-rounder in cricket who could win a place in a Test side by his fielding

There has been no greater entertainer in cricket than Learie Constantine. He drew record crowds in the Lancashire League and epitomised West Indian cricket with his fast bowling, furious hitting and dynamic fielding.

alone. Statistically, he has not the greatest of Test records, but his contribution to the game was enormous and his ranking among the world's greatest all-rounders is very high.

Constantine was the most dynamic figure in West Indian cricket in its formative years, and he established a pattern of speed, excitement and glorious entertainment which we have come to accept as the norm. He came to England in 1923 with H.B.G. Austin's team and won renown as a thrilling fielder at cover point. He was back in England in 1928 when he did the 'double', was recognised as one of the most exciting cricketers in the world, but did little in the three Test matches, West Indies' first, apart from taking 4 for 82 in the inaugural match at Lord's. One of his victims was Wally Hammond, then at his prime, whom he always troubled.

The match that set the cricket world buzzing on that tour was when the West Indians met Middlesex at Lord's at the beginning of June, two weeks before the first test. Middlesex declared at 352 for 6, and when Constantine went to the wicket on Monday the tourists, at 79 for 5, stood in danger of having to follow-on. 'In such a brilliant manner did he deal with the situation that, driving with great power, and pulling in daring fashion, he made 80 out of 107 in less than an hour.' The West Indians trailed by 122 on the first innings in spite of Constantine's effort. His part in the match had only just begun, however. When Middlesex batted again he took 7 for 57, his second spell realising 6 for 11 in 6.3 overs. He hit the stumps five times. Needing 259 to win, the West Indians looked sure to be beaten when they slipped to 121 for 5. Constantine now produced a display more sparkling than the one he had given in the first innings. He hit 2 sixes and 12 fours as he made 103 out of 133 in an hour. In attempting to stop one of his drives, J.W. Hearne so badly damaged a finger that he could not play again for the rest of the season. Constantine epitomised all that we have since come to expect from West Indian cricket – hard hitting, lightning bowling and thrilling fielding.

There was a feline characteristic in his fielding, both in anticipation and in quickness of movement. There was a ferocity in his bowling which gave Les Ames more trouble than any other bowler he encountered in Test cricket, and there was an elasticity in his batting. He would curl into a spring and explode with power as he unwound to hit the ball. Above all else he took the crowd with him. There was a murmur, a sitting up and a cheer whenever he came down the steps and a sense of sadness when he was out.

At the end of the 1928 tour he signed for Nelson in the Lancashire League. His efforts in the League were to bring it to the notice of a wider public. More than any other cricketer he became responsible for the League's immense popularity in the years before the war.

His forays into the first-class game were restricted, but always exciting, often dramatic. When West Indies beat England at Port of Spain in January 1935, and later took the series, he hit an explosive 90 and took 5 for 52 in the match. He had Leyland leg before off the penultimate ball of the match to win the game. He was one of the three fastest bowlers in the world at the time and was, in fact, cautioned in that match for excessive use of the bouncer.

It was appropriate that in the last Test match played before the outbreak of the Second World War, he should take 5 for 75, though now reduced in pace, and should hit a breathtaking 79. 'Constantine, in the mood suggesting his work in Saturday afternoon League cricket, brought a welcome air of gaiety to the Test arena. He revolutionised all the recognised features of cricket and, surpassing Bradman in his amazing stroke play, he was absolutely impudent in his aggressive treatment of bowling shared by Nichols and Perks. While the four remaining wickets fell those two bowlers delivered 92 balls from which Constantine made 78 runs out of 103. Seldom can there have been such a spreadeagled field with no slips, and Hammond did not dare risk further trouble by changing his attack. With an astonishing stroke off the back foot Constantine thumped Perks for 6 to the Vauxhall end – a very long carry – and helped himself to eleven 4's before he was last out to a very fine catch by Wood; running towards the pavilion the wicket-keeper held the ball that had gone high over his head.'

He studied Law while playing in the Lancashire League and was called to the Bar. He worked for the social services during the Second World War, wrote, broadcast and later returned to Trinidad where he became an MP. He returned to England as High Commissioner for Trinidad and Tobago, was awarded the MBE, knighted and made a Life Peer. He worked unceasingly, not just for the rights of black people as is frequently stated, but for the good of all humanity. The world was a lesser place when he died in 1971. Perhaps the greatest tribute of the many paid to him was in an essay by C. L. R. James: 'He did not leave the game as he found it. To very few has it been given to do this.'

Constantine showed what was possible; Gary Sobers achieved things on the cricket field that had seemed to be impossible. Of all the world's great all-rounders, he has been the most complete. He could bowl pace and spin, orthodox and experimental. He could bat at any number and field anywhere. He scored 8,032 runs in Test cricket, took 235 wickets and made 109 catches. He was of such exceptional talent that when one talks of him, muses on an innings or a shot one is inclined to forget the versatility of his bowling and the staggering breadth of his achievement as a bowler.

He was 17 when he was first picked to play for West Indies. He batted number nine, for he had been chosen as an orthodox slow left-arm bowler. His first wicket in Test cricket, as we have mentioned, was that of Trevor Bailey. He added three more in the innings, finishing with 4 for 75. England won by 9 wickets. That was April 1954. When the Australians travelled to the Caribbean the following year he had moved to number six in the order, scored consistently, opened upon one occasion and took wickets regularly. In New Zealand he batted at number three, always a good spot for a left-hander, and bowled much less.

On the tour to England in 1957 he played some entertaining all-round cricket, again opened in two Tests, but was part of a West Indian side that was well beaten and was in the process of being restructured. He looked an exciting prospect, but the emphasis was on promise rather than on performance. It was a few months after this tour that he first gave himself a permanent place in cricket history.

West Indies met Pakistan in a Test series for the first time. The first match, at Bridgetown, was drawn, but Sobers bowled 57 overs in the second innings as Hanif Mohammad scored 337 in 16 hours, 53 minutes. In the next Test, Sobers hit 52 and 80 as West Indies won by 120 runs. At Kingston, Jamaica, West Indies won by an innings. Sobers hit 365 not out, the highest score ever made in a Test match. It took him 10 hours, 14 minutes, which was more than three hours less than Hutton had taken over his 364 at The Oval in 1938. It was his first century in a Test match. He was 21 years old. Before he was to end his Test career he was to score another twenty-five Test hundreds, a number surpassed only by Bradman and Gavaskar. In fact, in the next Test, at Georgetown, he hit a hundred in each innings to bring his aggregate in his last three innings against Pakistan to 599 for once out.

Three more centuries followed in the series in India, and there were match figures of 6 for 65 in Madras. He was now viewed as an all-rounder of outstanding talent, although it was his batting which England feared most when they went to the Caribbean in January 1960. They had just cause to do so. In the first Test he scored 226, and he and Worrell added a record 399 for the fourth wicket. There were two more centuries and a 92 in the rubber, but England won the series. It was hard to believe that he was only 24.

Garfield Sobers – establisher of records, entertainer of crowds. Considered by many to be the greatest cricketer that the world has seen since the end of the Second World War.

In the tied Test which began the exhilarating 1960–61 series between Australia and West Indies, he hit 132. He had not begun the tour well, but 'Sobers hit himself out of an indifferent patch with a fine century in just over two hours on the first day of the first Test – some observers considered it to be the best hundred thay had ever seen – and he again found his touch at Sydney with 168, the highest Test innings for West Indies in the series.' He also took 15 wickets in the series. Of all the heroes of that summer, he was the one, after Worrell, whom the Australians most readily took to their hearts. He signed to play for South Australia in the Sheffield Shield for three seasons.

Twice in that period, 1961–64, he scored a thousand runs and took fifty wickets in a season, an amazing achievement. He had added a dimension to his bowling. His left-arm spin was of infinite variety. To the orthodox delivery he had added the ball out of the back of the hand with subtleties of disguise. He had bowled 41 eight-ball overs in succession in the final Test against Australia, taking 5 for 120, and his appetite for work never diminished as he changed to medium pace and above medium pace. He could move the ball prodigiously, and he became just about the best new ball bowler in the world to complement his unchallenged position as the best batsman, left or right-handed.

His three seasons with South Australia became legendary because, genial, modest, sporting and unassuming as he was, he always wanted to win. It mattered as much to him that South Australia beat New South Wales as it did that West Indies beat England or Australia. He was the cricketer in the world that people most wanted to see. As a crowd attraction only Grace and Botham among the great all-rounders can match him. There was excitement in the air with all that he did on the cricket field.

As a batsman he was technically supreme. Like all the greatest players his first movement was back. His pick-up was generous, his repertoire of shots total. He had that languid quality which made all look fluent and easy, and yet one was never surprised by the power which was ever brooding. He could be the most violent of hitters, uncoiling like a spring, as the world learned when he hit the slow left-arm of Malcolm Nash for six sixes in one over at Swansea in 1968. In 1971–72, at Melbourne, he scored 254 for the Rest of the World against Australia, and Don Bradman said that it was the best innings that he had ever seen. The Don is a kindly man, but he is not one to shower praise lightly.

Worrell brought his regrouped West Indian side to England in 1963 and won the series by three Tests to one. 'Sobers was the strong man of the party. He missed only six first-class engagements including the two played against Oxford and Cambridge, and in almost every game he played he contributed some outstanding performance. He left his imprint on every field he played, taking wickets at a vital time, making runs quickly when necessary and swallowing up 29 catches, mostly in the slips. His form in the last month of the tour qualified him as the outstanding all-rounder in present day cricket.' He averaged over 40 in the Tests and took 20 wickets. At Headingley he bowled only six overs in the first innings, but Worrell surprised everyone by withholding Wes Hall and giving the new ball to Sobers in the second innings. He produced alarming pace and swing and bowled Micky Stewart for a duck.

When Worrell stood down, Gary Sobers was the automatic choice for West Indies captain. He led his side to victory over Australia in Kingston on his first appearance as West Indies captain and celebrated the occasion by claiming his hundredth Test victim, Philpott. He had already scored over four thousand Test runs.

He was to lead West Indies in 39 successive Test matches, a record, and the drawn match with New Zealand at Port of Spain, April 1972, was his eighty-fifth match in succession for West Indies, a Test record which was later beaten by India's Viswanath. There was a certain tendency to gamble with his captaincy which did not please everybody, but there was always spice and flavour when Sobers was in charge. He led Nottinghamshire with great panache from 1968 until 1974. The county was very much in the doldrums until his arrival, but he breathed new life into them and won many friends on the county circuit. He scored more than seven thousand runs and took close to three hundred wickets for Notts, and interest in the county was stimulated. Rival supporters could never be quite sure whether they wanted to see him bat or wanted to see the back of him.

Sobers missed the 1972–73 series against Australia through a knee injury which was to trouble him for the rest of his career, but he came to England in the summer of 1973 under Kanhai's captaincy. At Lord's, in the third and final Test, he hit his last Test century, 150 not out as West Indies reached 652 for 8 declared. The picture of that exquisite cover drive rippling across the turf to the boundary, dissecting the field with a curve which was all part of the beauty of the stroke, remains etched in the memory, as will those gobbled catches at short-leg off the bowling of Lance Gibbs.

His last Test match came in Port of Spain a few months later. Surprisingly, the honours of the match went to Tony Greig and England, but in his ninety-third Test there was still time for Sobers to establish another record. When he had Amiss caught at slip in the first innings, it was his hundredth wicket against England.

Sobers had all the talents necessary for greatness as a cricketer. He had genius at the game and he combined it with an appetite for continued success and great stamina. He was as eager to score runs, take wickets and win matches in 1974 as he had been twenty years earlier. He accepted the intense adulation and publicity without it ever spoiling his modesty and enthusiasm. He was tall, he was strong and he was athletic, but above all there was joy in his every movement, and the crowd knew it. He was the culmination of West Indian liberation and the expression of that freedom and character through cricket. For C.L.R. James, the Caribbean's most noted cricket writer, 'his command of the rising ball in the drive, his close fielding and his hurling himself into his fast bowling are a living embodiment of centuries of a tortured history.'

More simply, at The Oval, when the West Indians were playing a few years ago, a Caribbean supporter turned to the present writer as Viv Richards was going out to bat and said, 'There's the king man. There goes the king.' And then he turned to look up at Sobers who was at the game and chatting on the balcony, and he added, 'And there's god up there!'

9

THE NEW BREED

The 1960s saw great changes in the structure of cricket with the introduction of the one-day game. The sixty-over knock-out cup competition, originally sponsored by Gillette, came into existence in 1963 and was followed six years later by the Sunday afternoon forty-over thrash, the John Player League. In 1972 the Benson and Hedges Cup, fifty-five overs an innings, zonal leagues leading to a knock-out tournament between eight counties, became the third one-day competition in English cricket. A year earlier, a rain-ruined Test match in Melbourne had brought about the birth of international limited-over cricket.

The common factor in all of these limited-over matches was that restrictions on the number of overs a player was allowed to bowl enforced sides to field at least five men who were capable of bowling. It was not necessary to bowl a team out to win a limited-over game, but to frustrate the other side in their efforts to score and to score quickly oneself. The all-rounder became the most important man in cricket, particularly if he could bowl medium pace and hit hard. The quality of the fifth bowler in a side could often make the difference between winning and losing, while the runs plundered in the last five or ten overs of an innings could again tip the balance in favour of one side.

Not only did the advent of the one-day game emphasise the importance of the all-rounder, it also created a new breed of men who could bat and bowl to advantage while athleticism in the field became of the utmost value. Oakman of Sussex, David Hughes of Lancashire, Johnson and Asif Iqbal of Kent, Tony Brown of Gloucestershire, Keith Boyce of Essex and West Indies, and John Steele and Brian Davison of Leicestershire were among those who prospered in the limited-over game.

Far from having the detrimental effect on cricketing prowess and technique which is normally ascribed to it, the one-day game has been a distinct advantage to and helped in the development of some cricketers. The prime example is in the case of Stuart Turner who represented Essex from 1965 to 1986. He was not re-engaged by the county after his debut season, but stirling performances in club cricket earned him a new contract in 1968. He bowled medium-fast, hit mightily and fielded outstandingly in any position. The arrival of the John Player League in 1969 played an important part in his life. He was not to miss a match on a Sunday afternoon until struck by injury in 1983, and when he retired at the end of the 1986 season he had scored more than three thousand runs and taken over three hundred wickets in the League.

One opponent commented of his bowling, 'When he started in county cricket he bowled just short of a length and you never felt in any danger against him. He bowled medium pace and you felt that you could play him all day long. But when the one-day game came along he became a different proposition. He was always nagging at you, and it was hard to get him away.'

The confidence gained by his success in the limited-over game spilled over into the county championship matches, and in 1974 he won the Cricket Society's Wetherall Award as the outstanding all-rounder in the country. He had scored 963 runs and taken 73 wickets in first-class cricket during the year. The Wetherall Award is one of the few attempts that has been made to recognise the worth of the all-rounder, and, after certain basic qualifications have been satisfied, it is determined by dividing the batting average by the bowling average. Winners in recent years have included Clive Rice, Richard Hadlee and Imran Khan.

Turner's career ended in the golden age of Essex cricket, for, in his last seven seasons, the county won all four of the major competitions, and he was an integral part of the success. There were those who believed that had he not been something of a rebel in his younger days, he would have played for England in a one-day international. That, however, was not to be, and he will be remembered only as an outstanding example of the quality all-round cricketer who came to the fore in the first-class game with the advent of one-day cricket.

It is worth noting that the great Gary Sobers played in only one limited-over international while Fred Titmus and Ray Illingworth appeared in only two and three respectively.

The careers of Titmus and Illingworth followed almost identical patterns. They both scored more than twenty thousand runs and took more than two thousand wickets in first-class cricket. They both passed a thousand runs and a hundred wickets in Test cricket. They both bowled off-spin, and they both played in the county championship at the age of 50. Titmus captained Middlesex for a time and was vice-captain of England; Illingworth captained Leicestershire and Yorkshire, and he was captain of England.

Balance and poise of one of the world's great off-spinners, Fred Titmus, who was also a good enough batsman to have opened for England.

Titmus played fifty-three Tests, beginning against South Africa at Lord's in 1955 and ending against Australia at Adelaide in 1975. Illingworth played in sixty-one tests. His first Test was against New Zealand at Old Trafford in 1958, and his last was against West Indies at Lord's in 1973 when Sobers hit his final Test hundred. Titmus did the 'double' eight times, Illingworth six.

Illingworth had great success as England's captain, bringing back the 'Ashes' from Australia and retaining them in a drawn series in England. He was also immensely successful as captain of Leicestershire whom he revitalised, steering them to two wins in the Benson and Hedges Cup, two in the John Player League and to the county championship. He returned to Yorkshire late in his career and was originally engaged as manager, but he took over the captaincy and led his side to the John Player League title.

Titmus was less successful as a captain and bitterly unlucky when he was vice-captain of England under Colin Cowdrey in the West Indies in 1967–68. He lost four toes when his foot was caught in the propeller of a motor boat, and, for a time, it was feared that his career was at an end, but the man's character and determination brought him back not only to Middlesex, but for a third tour of Australia with the England side of Australia in 1974–75.

Titmus was a master of flight and had a magnificent control of pace, his faster ball deceiving many batsmen and leaving them stumped Murray, bowled Titmus. In a period when the cricket world was rich in off-spin, he had no superior. His batting was courageous, founded on sound technique, and he was Boycott's first opening partner in a Test match. It was typical of this witty, cheerful, lively man that his best Test score, 84 not out, should come at a time when it was desperately needed. At Bombay, in 1964, England faced an Indian score of 300 without Barrington, Edrich and Sharpe, none of whom could play through injury, and without Stewart who withdrew after the match had started because of illness. Titmus batted number five, and England were 98 for 5, with Stewart unable to bat, but Titmus's tenacity took them to 233.

Ray Illingworth hit two Test hundreds, 113 against West Indies at Lord's in 1969, and 107 against India at Old Trafford two years later. He was a totally professional cricketer, and his batting reflected his attitude – stubborn, resourceful, tough and uncompromising. His attitude to the game was always combative, and it was his shrewdness and acute knowledge of cricket that made him such a fine leader. His off-spin bowling reflected his understanding of the game. It was flawlessly

One of the shrewdest of England captains, Ray Illingworth was an intelligent off-spinner and a most capable batsman. He was an all-rounder in every sense, for he knew the game fully.

accurate, probing at a batsman's weaknesses with subtlety of flight rather than excessive turn.

Titmus, Illingworth and David Allen of Gloucestershire, who did the 'double' in 1961 and was close to doing the 'double' in Test cricket, were the three bowlers who vied for the position of successor to Laker as England's off-spinner. Another Gloucestershire all-rounder, Mortimore, did the 'double' three times but never quite established himself as an off-spinner of Test quality. On occasions, Titmus, Allen and Illingworth were all in the same Test side, and frequently two out of the three played together. Initially, Titmus seemed the most likely bowler to succeed Laker, but Illingworth's success as captain gave him the edge in later years. The criticisms that were most generally levelled at Illingworth were that he tended to be negative at times, and that he was under-bowled, particularly in the period when he was captain.

Instinctively, the emphasis with Titmus and Illingworth has fallen on their bowling, and if one denies them a place as *great* all-rounders, it is because at Test level they were seen primarily as off-break bowlers who were very useful batsmen, but neither would have been chosen for an England side for his batting alone. Nevertheless, only nine players have scored twenty thousand runs and taken two thousand wickets in their careers, and Titmus and Illingworth are of that number. They represented the last of the great county all-rounders, the bread-and-butter men like Astill, Hopwood, Townsend, Kennedy and Horton who had come to the fore in the late 1920s and were at the heart of all first-class sides until the early 1960s. They were men of steel, humour, determination and unflinching endeavour, immensely popular among players and spectators, the most valuable men in cricket.

The international careers of Titmus and Illingworth were drawing to a close when England met Australia in the first limited-over international at Melbourne Cricket Ground on 5 January 1971, so was the Test career of Basil d'Oliveira who played in that match. Fate has decreed that d'Oliveira's name is best remembered for the courage and dignity he showed in overcoming so many obstacles to become an England cricketer. Had he been able to enter the Test arena sooner, it is likely that he would have ended with an all-round record as good as any in the game. It is significant that d'Oliveira played only four one-day internationals, for his talents in limited-over cricket helped Worcestershire to thrive in the early years of the one-day domestic competitions.

He was born in Cape Town, a Cape Coloured cricketer whose short back-lift was the product of the bad wickets on which he played his early cricket. It is likely, too, that those formative years contributed much to his great powers of concentration that were to stand him in such good stead later, but it should not be imagined for a moment that here was a dull batsman. He was relaxed and correct in style, and his powerful forearms gave a full range of strokes and the ability to score rapidly and attractively.

The laws of South Africa prevented him from testing his skills at the highest level in spite of his eighty centuries and hundreds of wickets obtained with his medium pace swing bowling, and in 1960 he came to England on a year's trial contract with Middleton in the Central Lancashire League. He ended the season ahead of Gary Sobers in the League averages. His fare to England had been paid by public subscription of those in Cape Town who supported him.

He toured Rhodesia with a Commonwealth side in 1961–62 and had his first taste of first-class cricket. On his second tour, Tom Graveney persuaded him that he had the ability to make the grade in county cricket and that he should join Worcestershire. He spent 1964 qualifying for the county, scoring a century against the touring Australians, and in 1965, his first full season, he passed 1,500 runs and took 38 wickets. Worcestershire won the county championship. A year later he was in the England side. He was 35 years old when he made his Test debut, an age at which Tony Greig's Test career had been over for four years.

His first Test wicket came when he bowled Seymour Nurse, and he hit 27 before he was run out. In the next Test he made 76 and 54, and he followed this with 88 at Headingley. The following season, he hit the first of his five Test centuries, 109 against India at Headingley.

His international career was to last until August 1972, when he played against Australia at The Oval. It was his forty-fourth Test, and he was 41 years old. In his Test career, he hit 2,484 runs, took 47 wickets and held 29 catches. When it is considered that he was, in all probability, denied some six or seven years of an international career by his need to move from South Africa, play in the Central Lancashire League and qualify for Worcestershire, and that he was rarely used as more than a fourth seamer and never took more than three wickets in a Test innings, d'Oliveira's record is quite remarkable. He scored nearly nineteen thousand runs and took nearly five hundred and fifty wickets in an abbreviated first-class career. His achievement was a fine one, but one is left with the perpetual question of what he might have accomplished had he been able to follow a first-class career in cricket from his youth.

The last series in which Basil d'Oliveira appeared witnessed the first appearance of Tony Greig, and if one entertains certain doubts as to

Greig's position in the world's great all-rounders, the reasons are not those that attend an assessment of d'Oliveira. On figures Greig cannot be faulted. In statistical terms he ranks second to Botham and above Rhodes, Bailey, Illingworth, Titmus and Tate among England's greatest Test all-rounders. Grace's golden days as a bowler were behind him when he began his Test career.

Greig was born in South Africa of a Scottish father and South African mother and came to Sussex in 1964 when he was still short of his 20th birthday. His first appearance in a county match was at the beginning of the 1967 season. Sussex were entertaining Lancashire at Hove, and when he went to the wicket his side were 34 for 3. Six feet, seven inches tall, fair and handsome, with a personality which instantly attracted the followers of the game, he hit 156 in four hours, savaging an attack that included Statham, Higgs and Peter Lever. By the end of the season he had scored well over a thousand runs and taken 67 wickets.

His height and his hair made him immediately recognisable wherever he went so that it was never necessary for anyone to ask, 'Which one is Greig?' when Sussex were in the field. He fielded well anywhere, and his medium pace bowling could always threaten because of the height from which he brought the ball down. As his career progressed he seemed to hold his bat higher and higher as the bowler ran in. He was the instigator of a stance since adopted by Gooch and others. In Greig's case it was born out of his height. There was a panache about him which attracted public attention, but he was always given to somewhat impetuous acts and statements which made many uneasy and gave the hint of the nonconformist below the charm.

He was eager to attack when he batted, and his style, essentially on the front foot, made him ever-ready to drive. He was a popular choice when chosen to play in the representative matches of 1970, England v Rest of the World, and he topped the bowling averages for this series in which he appeared three times. It was apparent that d'Oliveira would be pressed to hold his place, for Greig duplicated what d'Oliveira brought to the Test although his bowling was never to be as steady in spite of its success.

Greig's first test series marked d'Oliveira's last, as we have mentioned. His debut came in the first Test against Australia at Old Trafford, June 1972. He batted number six, which was always to be his favourite position, and was top scorer in both innings with 57 and 62. He dismissed Ian Chappell for a duck, and in Australia's second innings he took 4 for 53 as England won by 89 runs. By the end of the rubber, which was drawn, it was obvious that he not only had the temperament for the big occasion, but an insatiable appetite for it.

Tony Greig – a fierce competitor in all that he did.

He went to India with Tony Lewis's side in 1972–73, and was an outstanding success in the series, hitting the first of his eight Test centuries, topping the batting averages and finishing second in the bowling averages. After only two Test series he was established as an all-rounder of true international quality. *Wisden* was enthusiastic about him, but their correspondent Clive Taylor sounded a prophetic and a warning note. 'If he can temper his enthusiasm and so curb some of his mannerisms on the field which are too aggressive and embarrassing, he will probably go on to become England's captain.'

In fact, that event was only two years away and the evolutionary process which was to bring it about had already begun. At the conclusion of the tour of India and Pakistan Illingworth resumed the England captaincy with Lewis playing under him until forced out of the game through injury, but the twin series of 1973 saw the end of Illingworth's reign as England's captain. New Zealand were beaten, but England suffered at the hands of West Indies. In the last Test at Lord's, when West Indies made 652 for 8 declared, Greig had 3 for 180 from 33 overs, yet as the figures were read to the crowd over the public address system he raised his arms in triumph and they roared their approval in return. Like Miller before him and Botham after him, he demanded a response by his every act on the cricket field.

Mike Denness, England's vice-captain under Tony Lewis, led the side to the West Indies a few months later. The first Test saw Greig involved in his first major controversy. At the end of the second day, Bernard Julien played the last ball of the day back down the pitch. As the players relaxed and prepared to leave the field, Greig turned and seeing Kallicharran out of his ground, threw down the wicket at the bowler's end and appealed. The West Indian left-hander was given out. The incident caused a storm of protest and anger. There was much debate, and the appeal was withdrawn so that Kallicharran continued his innings next morning. It was a necessary action if the rubber were to continue in a tolerable atmosphere.

The third Test in Bridgetown saw Greig establish a record by becoming the first Englishman to score a century and take five wickets in an innings in the same Test match. Interestingly, his 46 overs which brought him 6 for 164 were composed mainly of off-spinners with which he had begun to experiment. The fourth Test brought him another century, and the fifth a personal triumph in an England victory which levelled the series. In the West Indian first innings he took 8 for 86, in the second 5 for 70 to bowl England to a 26-run win. On a worn wicket he had bowled quickish off-spinners and returned England's best figures by an England bowler against West Indies.

From the tour of Australia, 1974–75, he was one of the few men to emerge with credit. He was second in the batting averages, hit a sparkling hundred at Brisbane and no English bowler bettered his 17 wickets in the series. England were mauled by the ferocity of Lillee and Thomson, and there was criticism over the use of the bouncer at late order batsmen. John Thicknesse pointed out that it could have been Greig who was responsible for the way in which the tour developed: 'It might even be said that Greig was himself responsible for the slackening of the unwritten law that the ball should be pitched up to tailenders by dismissing Lillee with a bouncer at Brisbane in the first innings of the series.' Greig had a flair for the dramatic, and the reaction of an Australian crowd to his bowling a bouncer was sweet music to him. It was the song of battle.

He and Knott were the only men to play in all six Tests, and they alone stood out as the batsmen who could withstand Lillee and Thomson. They were responsible for eight of the scores of fifty or more, and 'Greig's flamboyance gave the side character in the field'.

Denness led England to the semi-final of the first World Cup, but he had been shattered by the pace of Lillee and Thomson in Australia, as had the rest of his side, and suffered a further reverse when England were beaten by an innings at Edgbaston after he had chosen to field first. John Edrich had been vice-captain in Australia, but it was Tony Greig who was named as Denness's successor when the Kent man was replaced. His debut as England's captain was characteristically spectacular. Lillee and Thomson had reduced England to 49 for 4 when he went in. He hit 96 in two and a half hours. England did not lose again during the series. Tony Greig stood at the summit of popularity. His height, his looks and his flamboyant approach to the game won him recognition from a television-viewing public, some of whom had never been inside a cricket ground.

He greeted the arrival of the West Indies the following year with the statement that England would make them 'grovel'. West Indies did not grovel. They won three of the five Tests and two were drawn. They had the best record of any West Indian side that had been to England, yet Greig's reputation as an inspiring leader was unimpaired. Interviewed on television at the end of the series about his 'grovel' comment, he laughed and shrugged it off. Everybody laughed with him.

He took a reshaped side to India. Barlow, John Lever, Randall, Brearley and Roger Tolchard were among those making their first tours for England. In the second Test, Greig scored one of the slowest of Test centuries, but he became the first England player to reach a 'double' of three thousand runs and a hundred wickets in Test cricket. England won a rubber in India for the first time in thirty-three years. Greig had been an immense success both on and off the field.

From India, England travelled to Melbourne for the Centenary Test. It was a triumph in every way, and Greig made a considerable contribution to its success as a match and as a social occasion. From that point his decline was as rapid and poignant as his rise had been exciting and dramatic. While England's captain, he was secretly negotiating with some of the best players in the world on behalf of the Packer organisation. He was using a position of authority and trust conferred upon him by the T.C.C.B. and the England selectors to further the aims of an organisation bent on disrupting the structure and well-being of traditional cricket. He was sacked from the England captaincy in an air of bitterness and bewilderment, but, on the insistence of his successor, Brearley, he was retained in the side.

His activities for Mr Packer and his commitment to World Series Cricket lessened his involvement with the game in England. In 1978 Sussex released him from his contract and he settled in Australia to become a high-powered executive in the Packer empire of television and marketing. What had once been seen as humour and panache, people now saw as cynicism and contempt. It was reflected that, in four years as captain of Sussex, he had promised much and achieved nothing. His clandestine actions cast a shadow on all that had gone before. There were many traditional followers of the game who felt that they had been duped, that it had all been a charade, a smoke-screen for some greater commercial gain. Never had an idol fallen so far. In retrospect, one can consider that cricket had been in need of a shake-up and that ordinary county players have benefited from the changes that came about. One can also note that it stimulated the interest of new sponsors for Test and county cricket, but nothing will ever excuse how World Series Cricket was brought into being nor persuade people that the motives behind it were anything other than personal profit.

From the moment of his association with the Packer project, Greig's own cricketing performances fell away although he was only 31 years old, but his Test match record remains mightily impressive. He was a cricketer of fire and passion, the most combative of all-rounders. He was a better batsman than he was a bowler, and he was always at his best in a crisis, relishing the fight. His height, which was an advantage to him as a batsman, did not help him in maintaining control as a bowler. This was less obvious in his medium pace bowling, but more apparent when he turned to spin. He had his days of glory, notably the one in Port of Spain, but there have been very few tall men who have been good slow bowlers, and only Sobers has really been of Test class as both a quick and a slow bowler.

The key to the hesitation one has in a final assessment of Greig's quality as an all-rounder of the highest class lies in the statistics of his career. His record in Test matches was infinitely better than his overall career record. This would suggest that Greig was essentially a big occasion player, that he was the first of a growing line who perform outstandingly in the international arena while showing moderate form in county cricket. Grace, Rhodes, Jackson, Hirst and Bailey were not of this failing.

Greig's last Test series was against Australia in 1977. He scored 0 and took 1 for 17 in his last appearance in Test cricket, but Brearley's men had by then regained the 'Ashes'. Greig had appeared in fifty-eight consecutive Tests. His last series was the one in which Boycott reached his hundredth hundred, and in the third match a young all-rounder named I.T. Botham made his Test debut.

10

THWARTED GENIUS

One of the positive aspects of Kerry Packer's World Series Cricket is that it gave an opportunity for South African cricketers of outstanding ability, who were denied Test cricket for political reasons, to display their talents in international competition.

South Africa has a long tradition of fine all-round cricketers. It began with Aubrey Faulkner who accomplished a remarkable 'double' when he toured England in 1912, remarkable in that he adapted so readily to foreign wickets at a time when cricket in South Africa was played on matting. His debut in Test cricket had come at Johannesburg in January 1906, when he had match figures of 6 for 61 with his leg-breaks and googlies and South Africa won a Test match for the first time.

South Africa won that series against England by four Tests to one, and although they did not win in England in 1907 they impressed all with their ability and zest. None made a greater impression than Faulkner who took 6 for 17 in eleven overs in the Test match at Headingley. His batting, although a little ungainly, made considerable strides and he passed a thousand runs on the tour, opening on several occasions.

He was even more deadly with his bowling when South Africa entertained England in 1909–10 and won the series by three Tests to two. He took 29 wickets in the five Tests and topped the batting averages by a wide margin, hitting 123 in the first match and 99 in the last.

Visiting Australia a year later, when South Africa were well beaten, he scored 204 in the second Test in Melbourne. This was the first double century scored for South Africa in Test cricket and was to remain a record for twenty-five years. In the series, he hit 732 runs and was again the outstanding South African cricketer.

He served with distinction in the First World War and settled in England where he opened a cricket school in London which won international renown. He played club cricket in Nottinghamshire with much success, but his greatest performance in England came at Eastbourne in 1921.

Warwick Armstrong's great Australian side were unbeaten, but at the beginning of the year the veteran MacLaren had vowed that he could turn out a side to beat them. Having won eight and drawn two of their last ten Tests against England, the Australians came to the Saffrons to meet MacLaren's amateur eleven. MacLaren's boast seemed an embarrassingly vain one when his side was bowled out for 43, but bowling of the highest quality by Gibson and Faulkner, who took 4 for 50, restricted the Australian first innings lead to 131. Faulkner then played a defiant innings of 153, taming Gregory, Macdonald and Armstrong, and leaving the Australians 196 to win. At lunch on the last day, they were 87 for 5, but in the half an hour after lunch, Andrews and Ryder scored 34. The score was 140 for 5 when MacLaren brought on Faulkner in place of Falcon who had been expensive. It was Gibson, however, who broke the stand by having Ryder caught, but it was Faulkner who delivered the decisive blow when he knocked back Andrew's off-stump with a ball which whipped across the wicket from leg. The score was 153 for 8, with Armstrong himself still at the crease, but he was no match for Faulkner. 'Armstrong's struggles with Faulkner were pathetic; he merely lunged at the ball when it was in the air, lost it as it spun, then desperately changed his stance at the last minute.' Armstrong was leg before, and MacLaren's side won by 28 runs.

Faulkner was his own theorist in his pioneering coaching, and many famous cricketers benefited from his advice and instruction. He was a man of restless endeavour with a highly strung temperament, and tragically he took his own life in 1930 when he was only 48. He was the criterion by which later South African all-rounders were to be judged.

The only South African to better Faulkner's record of 1,754 runs and 82 wickets in Test cricket is Trevor Goddard who, with 2,516 runs and 123 wickets, established a record which, with South Africa's exclusion from Test cricket, is unlikely to be broken in the foreseeable future.

Trevor Goddard was a left-handed batsman of sound technique, a medium pace left-arm bowler of unrelenting nagging accuracy and an excellent close to the wicket fielder. His rise to the top in South African cricket was unspectacular, the natural progression of a young man who was technically correct and highly proficient in all that he did. He was diligent in application, quietly confident and eager of promotion. He did not win a place in the Natal side until 1952–53, however, when

Trevor Goddard, the outstanding South African all-rounder of his generation. A most durable cricketer.

Cheetham's party was on tour in Australia. In his second match, he hit 100 not out as Natal beat Eastern Province by an innings in Durban.

This innings focused public attention upon him. It was an outstanding achievement by a young man of 21 who was batting at number seven and opening the bowling. More brave efforts followed, particularly at Newlands, Cape Town, where Western Province, the eventual winners of the Currie Cup, set Natal to make 366 in their second innings. 'The veteran Nourse and Goddard in a magnificent partnership almost brought off the impossible.' After they were separated, Natal collapsed and were beaten by 21 runs.

The satisfaction of his first season success in the Currie Cup began to evaporate for Goddard in 1954. Natal were back to full strength with the return of their Test players. Goddard's opportunities to play an innings became fewer, while all that seemed to be required of him as a bowler was that he should send down a couple of overs to get the shine off the ball so that Hugh Tayfield and Ian Smith could operate more effectively with their spinners. His frustration grew so acute that he contemplated giving up first-class cricket.

The change in fortune came when Natal played the New Zealand tourists in November 1953. Goddard was asked to open with McGlew, and although he was not an immediate success, it was the beginning of a most fruitful partnership. He ended the season as top of the Natal batting averages, hitting 174 against Western Province, and captured 9 wickets in his 75 economic overs.

A year later his all-round worth was recognised and he was selected in the South African party which toured England under Jack Cheetham in 1955. This was the first rubber to be played in England in which each match produced a definite result. England won the first two Tests, South Africa the next two, and England clinched the series with a win at The Oval. Goddard opened with McGlew in all five Tests, and he also opened the bowling in the first and last Tests. It was a most auspicious first series in Test cricket for the newcomer. His 25 wickets placed him only one behind Tayfield who had established a South African record. In all the matches he took 60 wickets and scored 1,163 runs. Six feet, two inches tall and very determined, he was essentially defensive in his approach to the game. His batting was founded on survival, and his bowling was aimed at or outside the leg stump to a packed leg side field. It was not particularly attractive, but it was effective, and he was the most successful South African all-rounder since Faulkner.

He was now an automatic choice for the Test side. He played in all five

Tests against May's team in 1956–57 and was ever-present against Craig's Australians a year later. In the first Test, he and McGlew created a record opening stand against Australia with a partnership of 176. Goddard made 90. In the second innings of the second Test, at Newlands, he carried his bat, making 56 not out as South Africa were bowled out for 99.

His success in domestic cricket in South Africa was consistent, and he grew in stature season by season. In December 1959, Natal played Border at East London and were bowled out for 90. Goddard then bowled 11 overs, took 6 for 3, and Border were all out for 16, the lowest total in the history of the Currie Cup. They were to make 18 in the second innings. The *South African Cricket Annual* reported: 'Goddard's tremendous performance, assisted no doubt by the state of the wicket, was the result of intelligent bowling. This is the third occasion 6 wickets have been taken by a South African for less than double figures, and for good measure he included his first hat trick in his performance.' A month later he scored 200 against Rhodesia.

On his second tour to England, in 1960, he was vice-captain to McGlew. This was a miserable tour. There were anti-apartheid demonstrations wherever the South Africans went. They were no match for England as a team, and the summer was wet. Added to these woes was the throwing controversy caused by fast bowler Griffin's suspect action. Nevertheless, Goddard survived well. He topped a thousand runs for the tour and took 73 wickets. He scored 99 in the fifth Test at The Oval, and with 17 wickets was second to Adcock. His cricket still lacked adventure, however, and it was felt that he had made little progress since 1955. 'Brought up in modern cricket he lacked initiative.'

He missed the home series against New Zealand, 1962–63, but captained South Africa creditably in the drawn rubber in Australia a year later. Goddard had missed the Tests against New Zealand because he and his wife, who was English, had settled in England for a while. Goddard played for Great Chell in the North Staffordshire League while he was in England, and his experiences as a League professional transformed his attitude as a cricketer. He broke Frank Worrell's record in the League, and his 64 wickets placed him second to Sonny Ramadhin. Where once there had been solidity and an emphasis on defence which bordered on stagnation, there was now a fresh approach born of the demands of the League which were forceful and responsible. In South Africa, on his return, they found him almost unrecognisable. He hit four centuries, averaged 86·71, took wickets economically and Natal won the Currie Cup.

He was asked to captain the side to Australia in 1963–64 after others had declined, McLean and van Ryneveld having been the first choices. His appointment coincided with the introduction to the South African side of some exciting young players like Barlow, who had opened in Goddard's absence, and Graeme Pollock. Creditable though his performances in Australia were, there was still the opinion that he was too wary in his approach. His own play had become more positive, but his leadership of the side still bordered on the tentative. Louis Duffus, the South African writer, touched on the point when he wrote: 'On the field Goddard was too considerate to his players, too reluctant to hurt their feelings, to urge them to speed up when they were fatefully defensive. His attitude was that they were adults and quite capable of knowing how to construct their innings. He gave them no instructions and more than once lack of impetus brought the team negative results.'

Nevertheless, he was reappointed captain when Mike Smith's England side arrived in South Africa the following season. It was a disappointing series. England won the first Test and were content to draw the rest. Goddard had the satisfaction of scoring his first Test century, but his lack of enterprise as a captain blighted what chances his side had of levelling the series. It was suggested to him that he should stand down as captain, for the responsibility of leadership could be affecting his play. He was hurt by the suggestion and, though he declined to stand down, he announced that he would retire from first-class cricket at the end of the series. The restriction on leg side field placings had rendered his bowling less effective, and it was as if he were out of joint with the times.

He was offered the captaincy of the South African side which came to England in 1965 on a three-Test tour and won, but he refused the invitation and Peter van der Merwe led the team with excitement and inspiration. South Africa had jettisoned its negative approach to the game, and under van der Merwe a new and exciting era dawned. It was a golden age of South African cricket, if a brief one.

In fact, Goddard continued to play first-class cricket and in 1966–67 he enjoyed his finest season. He had moved to North Eastern Transvaal who were captained by the excellent Glamorgan all-rounder Jim Pressdee. In his temporary retirement Goddard had been employed as a coach with the Sports Foundation. Like many others, he found that coaching young people made him consider his own game, and his batting took on a new aggression while his bowling was no longer slanted towards the leg stump. He hit 830 runs and took 45 wickets. He was seen as the perfect balance to the young, enthusiastic players now in the national side, particularly fast bowler Peter Pollock. After much persuasion Goddard agreed to return to Test cricket and to play against the visiting Australians.

The start to the series was sensational. Australia led by 126 on the first innings at Johannesburg, but South Africa hit 620 in their second attempt. On the last day Trevor Goddard took 6 for 53 in 32.5 overs, and South Africa had beaten Australia for the first time in a Test match in South Africa. It was the best bowling performance of Goddard's Test career. Australia drew level by winning the second Test, but the series went to South Africa with two more wins. Goddard hit 74 and 59 in the fifth Test and finished the series with 26 wickets at 16.23 apiece. He was a hero again.

When the Australians returned to South Africa three years later they were completely outplayed by a side that was now the best in the world. Barry Richards and Lee Irvine had joined a team that was led by Ali Bacher. Goddard was again pressed into service. He was now 38, but he had always trained hard and was superbly fit. He was Richards's opening partner in the first three Tests, but he was more successful with the ball than with the bat. In the third Test, at Johannesburg, he bowled South Africa to victory by 307 runs when he took 3 for 27 in 24.5 overs in the second innings. He ended the match when he had Connolly caught at slip by Richards. It was the last ball he bowled in Test cricket. He had told the selectors that he was not available for the tour of England and so he was omitted from the fourth and final Test. He is in the record books as the only South African to have done the 'double' in Test cricket, and his 48 catches have been surpassed by only one other South African fielder, Bruce Mitchell.

Goddard will never be remembered as one of the most exciting of players, but few worked harder, and he was a totally dedicated and very fit all-rounder. He played much of his cricket in a dull period of South African, and Test, cricket, and it was happy that he should be part of his country's golden age at the end of his career.

The Test match at Port Elizabeth in March 1970 from which Goddard was omitted was, in fact, South Africa's last appearance on the international scene before their excommunication from Test cricket. The tour of England on which Goddard had declined to go never took place. It was hastily replaced by an international series, England v Rest of the World. There were five South Africans in the Rest of the World side, and the one who took the honours was a tough, bespectacled all-rounder named Eddie Barlow.

Eddie Barlow who inspired Derbyshire by deeds and in leadership. He was a tenacious cricketer as batsman, bowler and fielder.

In those now forgotten contests, Barlow scored centuries at Lord's and Trent Bridge, and finished top of the bowling averages with 20 wickets at 19·80 runs each. At Headingley, he took 7 for 64 with 4 wickets in 5 balls including the hat trick.

Eddie Barlow was to become familiar and immensely popular in England. He joined Derbyshire in 1976, took over the captaincy in his first season and revitalised the county, taking them to a final at Lord's and leaving them after three years a sharper and more entertaining side. He breathed a will to win into them.

He played Currie Cup cricket for Eastern and Western Province, Transvaal and Boland, and an impressive Test career was cut short by the ban on South Africa. His first chance in Test cricket came when Goddard was unavailable for the series against New Zealand, 1961–62, and he soon established himself as a stocky, pugnacious opening batsman, strong off the back foot and solid in defence. Two years later he became the first South African to score centuries in his first two Tests against Australia. Later in the series he hit 201 at Adelaide. Goddard used his bowling sparsely in those Tests, but in the match at Adelaide, he followed his double century with 3 for 6.

His success with the bat continued when he played successive innings of 71, 15, 138, 78, 96 and 42 against Mike Smith's England team the following year. It was not until the Australians came to South Africa in 1966–67 that his right-arm fast-medium pace bowling with clever changes of pace and prodigious swing began to be used more fully, and he took 15 wickets in the series, including 5 for 85 at Cape Town.

When the Australians returned in 1969–70 he batted in the middle order in the first three Tests and hit two centuries. After that South African triumph the curtain came down, and Barlow was left with an abbreviated Test career – 30 appearances, 2,516 runs, 40 wickets, 35 catches.

He had a further taste of international competition when he played in World Series Cricket, but nothing will ever compensate for those lost years. He was 30 when his Test career was brought to an end. He had scored six centuries in Tests, and Goddard's all-round record was well within his reach. He was a supremely confident cricketer and his burly frame bristled with endeavour.

A modest, charming, courteous and friendly man, he is Director of the South African Sports Office in London, and he has argued the case for South Africa's return to Test cricket with a balance and honesty which even those who oppose his view have respected with warmth.

If Barlow was deprived in playing only thirty Tests when more may have been expected, then what of Michael John Procter who was only 24 when South Africa were banned from Test cricket and had played but seven Test matches. Those seven Tests were all against Australia in South Africa. The first of them was at Durban in January 1967, when he took 3 for 27 and 4 for 71. The last four came when the Australians returned under Lawry in 1969–70, and South Africa won all four Tests. Procter devastated the opposition with his pace. Charging in like a raging bull and delivering the ball before the front foot landed with a twirl of the arms like a windmill, Procter generated speed that was unmatched in his prime by all save Lillee. In that last series he took 26 wickets at 13·57 runs apiece, and his Test record was an incredible 41 wickets at 15·02. He did not score a Test fifty, for in that South African side he batted in the lower part of the order and it was his bowling that was needed, but he still averaged 25·11 from his ten Test innings.

One can think of only Compton, Sobers, Viv Richards and Botham who have so magnetised a crowd since the war. Mike Procter was a dynamic player of constant endeavour. If his bowling was unorthodox, his batting was classical, essentially front foot, leading from a solid base to a mighty crescendo.

He was a schoolboy protégé, excelling at every sport. He scored centuries from the age of 11 onwards, and he came to England with the South African Schools team in 1963. Gloucestershire noticed him. He returned in 1965 to qualify for them, and from 1968 to 1981 he played for the western county. He captained them from 1977 until his departure.

Of all the overseas players who have been attached to English counties since the Second World War, none has been so readily accepted by the followers of a county, none has become such an integral part of a county, nor identified himself so wholeheartedly with those whom he represented. The term 'Proctershire' was not given to Gloucestershire in the 1970s simply because he was a dominant cricketer, but also because of his total and obvious commitment to the county.

In an English first-class season which had become shortened by the proliferation of one-day cricket, he twice passed one hundred wickets and nine times scored more than a thousand runs. For the last years of his career in England he was troubled by a knee injury, but nothing ever stopped him from giving all that he had, especially when his side was under pressure.

He was shy, retiring and taciturn when he first came to Gloucestershire, but he gradually became at one with those around him. He would stroll round the ground at Bristol with his baby in his arms, chatting easily to the Gloucestershire supporters for whom he remains a legend on a par with Wally Hammond, Tom Goddard, Charlie Barnett or Tom Graveney.

Just under 6 feet tall, solid and strong of build, he was an all-rounder who was capable of transforming a match with an innings or an over. He twice took Gloucestershire close to winning the county championship. In 1976 their game with Worcestershire was abandoned without a ball being bowled so that they were pointless, but they finished only 24 points behind Middlesex who won the title. The next year they had two matches abandoned without a ball being bowled and they finished only five points behind Middlesex and Kent.

The 1977 season was, however, a memorable one for Gloucestershire. They fought their way to the semi-final of the Benson and Hedges Cup where they were drawn to play the strong Hampshire side at Southampton.

Mike Procter, Gloucestershire and South Africa. He gave everything to his side and to those who came to watch.

Gloucestershire were restricted to 180, but within a few overs of the start of the Hampshire innings that looked a massive total. 'All was overshadowed by a tremendous individual peformance by Procter, the Gloucestershire captain, who ripped away the Hampshire front-line batting by taking their first four wickets in five balls, including a hat trick. At full pace, Procter bowled Greenidge with the fifth ball of his third over. Then he dismissed Richards, Jesty and Rice with the first three balls of his fourth.' The first two of the hat trick, Barry Richards and Trevor Jesty, were leg before to Procter who was bowling round the wicket. David Turner and Nigel Cowley effected a recovery, but Procter returned to take two more wickets, and Gloucestershire won by 7 runs. Procter won the Gold Award. His figures were 6 for 13 in 11 overs, five of which were maidens. A splendid team effort, 'inspired by their splendid captain, Procter', took Gloucestershire to an easy win over the more favoured Kent in the final.

The hat trick was nothing new to Procter. He performed the hat trick against Essex at Westcliff in 1972, and at Southend in 1977, and in 1979 he did it twice, against Leicestershire at Bristol, and against Yorkshire at Cheltenham. Those last two hat tricks were obtained in successive matches. Against Leicestershire he also hit 122 and had a spell of 5 for 1, while against Yorkshire, bowling at full pace round the wicket, he had Lumb, Athey and Hampshire leg before with successive deliveries.

As the years advanced and his knee troubled him, he would bowl offbreaks more often than not, turning the ball sharply. Only Sobers bettered him with success at both pace and spin.

Procter is the only man in the history of the game to have performed the hat trick and hit a hundred in the same match twice, for he had accomplished this against Essex in 1972, and his figures against Worcestershire in 1977 were 108 and 13 for 73. Three years later he scored 73 and 35 against them and took 14 for 76.

He had the qualities which most captivate a crowd. He bowled at a furious pace and he hit ferociously hard. Yet to think of him as a mere hitter is a total misconception of the standard of his batting which was of the very highest class. He played for Natal, Western Province and Rhodesia in the Currie Cup in South Africa, and it was for Rhodesia that he made his highest score of 254. That double century brought him equal to a world record set up by C. B. Fry and Don Bradman. He had begun the season of 1970–71 with 119 against Natal 'B'. This was followed by 129 against Transvaal 'B', 107 against Orange Free State, 174 against North Eastern Transvaal and 106 against Griqualand West, so that the double century against Western Province was his sixth century in succession.

Records tumble over each other when we talk of Mike Procter, but his former colleague, Somerset secretary and England manager Tony Brown, says that they meant nothing to him. 'He wasn't interested in records or what he'd done. He gave everything to the side. If we needed a quick fifty or a quick wicket or two, that's what he'd try to provide. He was never interested in a hundred if Gloucestershire only needed thirty or forty from him. What a man!'

He relished the chance to play international cricket again of a sort when Packer came along and he has remained a staunch supporter of World Series Cricket because of the opportunity it gave to him and Eddie Barlow and Barry Richards to test themselves against other players of international standing. He played for South Africa against the South African Breweries team led by Graham Gooch although nearing forty and troubled by his knee injury. He was then forced to retire, but even at the time of writing, one hears that he is itching to have a go at Hughes's Australians. It is typical of the man, but even he must bow to the passing and wear-and-tear of the years.

In his history of Gloucestershire, Grahame Parker ends with a chapter entitled quite poignantly 'Nothing is Forever'. Almost his last words are of Procter: 'So Mike Procter, the greatest match winner in the history of the Club, had limped off the Road in 1981. His tempestuous career in every dimension of the game was over. His figures for Gloucestershire are 14,441 runs, 833 wickets and 185 catches, but cold statistics can never relate to the excitement of watching him bat and bowl. Never again would we see that long run gathering momentum to the mid air explosive blast at the wicket. Cricket is the poorer with his passing.'

Had he been permitted to sustain a Test career, what deeds he might have wrought.

11

THE NOTTINGHAMSHIRE DUO

In 1971, the year that Procter completed his six centuries in succession, Clive Rice was selected as one of South Africa's five cricketers of the year. It was the culmination of only two seasons in first-class cricket which had seen him rise from the Transvaal 'B' eleven in his first year to first change bowler and number six batsman in the Transvaal Currie Cup winning side the next season. His figures were professional and workmanlike, 202 runs, average 22·44, and the highest number of wickets, 21, at 18·33. His rise through the Transvaal School XI, Natal University and Old Johannians Club was steady rather than spectacular, but as a bowler of above medium pace and a batsman with a full range of shots and an eagerness to attack allied to a sound technique, he was recognised by the *cognoscenti* as an all-rounder of outstanding talent. He was selected to tour Australia in 1971–72, but that tour never took place. The door to Test cricket was closed to him before his career began.

Frustrated and initially embittered by his country's exclusion from Test cricket, Rice joined Ramsbottom in the Lancashire League in an effort to enhance his future in the game. In 1973 his club were beaten by two points for the title, but he won high praises from the League's chronicler, John Kay. 'Ramsbottom kept on East Lancashire's heels throughout the season, because in Clive Rice from South Africa, they had one of the most successful recruits to the League. Rice contributed 531 runs and took 66 wickets to arouse the interest of several county clubs as well as the envy of most of his side's opponents. A talented cricketer and a likeable one, Rice did much to revive Ramsbottom's reputation for fighting cricket.'

'At the time,' says Rice, 'I had no intention of playing county cricket, but Jack Bond saw me in a festival match and asked me if I was the Clive Rice who played in the Lancashire League. I said that I was, and he offered me a job with Notts in succession to Gary Sobers. There had been tentative approaches from elsewhere, but the challenge of following Sobers was what attracted me.'

He joined Nottinghamshire in 1975 and was an immediate success. In spite of hamstring trouble, he scored over a thousand runs and topped the bowling averages with more than fifty wickets. It marked the beginning of a fine period in Nottinghamshire's history. Sobers had made the county attractive and drawn people to watch them, but they had never seriously challenged for the championship – in 1973 they had finished last, and in 1974 third from bottom. Thereafter they were to climb steadily.

Rice became a major influence on Nottinghamshire and on the game itself. His dedication and professionalism became a model for those around him, and he is still angered when he sees a lack of application in any player. He sometimes despairs of the attitude of fellow professionals.

The improvement in Nottinghamshire's fortunes came to a halt in 1977 when they again finished bottom of the county championship. No blame could be attached to Rice. He was the winner of the Wetherell Award as the season's outstanding all-rounder. 'Rice enjoyed his best season in English cricket. Having thrown off the shackles of injury, he provided a brilliant inspiration to the team which, unfortunately, proved incapable of backing him up. He finished top of the batting and bowling averages not only in first-class games but in one-day competition as well. Without Rice Nottinghamshire cricket would have been a shambles and it was good news for the county when he signified his intention to renew his contract.' He was also appointed captain for 1978, Notts seeing in his leadership the intelligence and flair which could lead them from the doldrums.

Before this appointment could be put to the test there were dramatic developments. Rice returned from South Africa, announced that he had agreed to play in the World Series Cricket which Packer was organising for the winter of 1978–79. None could blame him for grasping at the opportunity to play against international competition, and he was backed by the South African authorities, but Notts dismissed him instantly and reappointed Smedley as captain who had led the side in 1977. Throughout the following weeks of disarray Rice maintained the calm and dignity which has been a feature of his cricket and his life. He attended the Cricket Society function at the Empire Rooms, Tottenham Court Road, to collect the Wetherell Award before returning to Nottingham early in support of Hassan's benefit. He spoke without rancour of his dismissal by Notts, his desire to continue to play for them and his reasons for joining the Packer style of cricket. Later he sought redress in the High Court, but Notts had a change of heart and reinstated him as a player, although not as captain.

The affair had had a beneficial effect for Notts. As a replacement for Rice they signed Richard Hadlee who, in effect, could play in only six championship matches because of the New Zealand tour of England in 1978. These six matches were enough to show that he and Rice would make a formidable pair. They became friends, and they lifted Notts to great heights with their skill and endeavour.

Finding himself back in the county side in 1978, Clive Rice hit 1,871 runs, average 66·82, and topped the national averages. He also took 41 wickets at 21·36 runs each. As the season progressed he was troubled by a shoulder injury and was unable to bowl as much as he would have liked. Notts rose to seventh in the table, and Clive Rice was named as cricketer of the year.

Rice again performed well in 1979, but more strange events overtook Notts. Ken Taylor, in his first season as manager of the county, decided that the side needed more positive and aggressive captaincy than was being shown by Smedley, and the captain was deposed on the eve of a Gillette Cup match with Warwickshire in July and Rice appointed in his place. The manner of this action caused as much stir as Rice's initial rejection, but, as local reporter John Lawson commented, Rice's 'all-round brilliance and ruthless attitude were his chief credentials'. Ruthless seems too harsh a word to apply to such a polite and gentle man, but on the cricket field he has a determination to win which few can match. It is the lack of the desire to win and the complacent attitude towards practice and improvement in many county players which is what troubles him most about the game in England.

Ken Taylor's action was vindicated when Notts rose to third in the county championship in 1980. It was the highest position that they had occupied for fifty-one years, and the success was due to Rice's leadership as well as his personal skill which saw him finish just short of 1,500 runs and take 39 wickets. Again he was troubled by injury, and he did not have the support of Hadlee who was also injured, but he was named as one of *Wisden*'s five cricketers of the year.

It is sad that he has been hampered by injury, for his bowling took him to the top of the averages in South Africa, and until slowed in 1984, Clive Rice was quick. He could generate pace from a strong action, and he still swings the ball away from the bat with a late movement that troubles all batsmen. His length has remained immaculate, but there was a time when he and Hadlee brought back memories of Larwood and Voce to Trent Bridge. His batting has been unimpaired by the injury that affected his

Clive Rice. A man of the utmost integrity. His example as a cricketer and as a man is one which young players in the game would do well to follow.

shoulder. He is a powerful, front-foot driver, but his magnificent hitting is never a violation of technique.

The mention of Larwood and Voce is not ill-judged, for in 1981, it was reported that 'Not since the days of Harold Larwood and Bill Voce had Trent Bridge hosted such celebratory scenes as those that greeted Nottinghamshire's final victory of the season over Glamorgan. The win – the ninth in their last eleven games of the summer – gave them the county championship for the first time in 52 years.'

Hadlee hit 745 runs and took 105 wickets in the championship and played a major part in the Notts success. 'It was,' said *Wisden*, 'a personal triumph for both men, particularly the South African, Rice, who, having been denied the opportunity of displaying his considerable talents on the Test scene, revealed a single-minded determination to lead Nottinghamshire to eventual victory. His all-round play led to his being labelled as the most complete player in world cricket, Botham included. Rice scored 1,462 runs at an average of 56·23 and his positive and vibrant leadership created winning situations where none seemingly existed.' He also took 65 wickets.

If one looks for a measure to decide who is the most complete player in world cricket then the Silk Cut Challenge tried to provide it. The competition between the world's leading all-rounders was first staged at Taunton in 1984. Botham, Marshall, Kapil Dev, Hadlee and Rice each batted for sixteen overs and bowled four overs at each of the opponents. The batsman's score was to be divided by the number of times he was out and then multiplied by the number of wickets that he took, so that if he failed to take a wicket his total would be nought.

Rice battled through his sixteen overs and scored 73 without being dismissed. He then proceeded to put Marshall out of the competition by getting him out four times. Botham launched a violent attack on Rice, but under the rules of the competition, which Rice had studied carefully, the battering made no difference to the bowler. Rice finished the day with seven wickets so that his point total was 511. Kapil Dev, with 117, was the closest to this. Clive Rice received £6,000 and the Silver Challenge Cup as the reward for being the world's greatest all-rounder.

There was a feeling that it was not a fair judge of the players concerned, and when the seven competitors arrived at Arundel for the 1985 competition spread over two days the rules had been changed. Rice, Hadlee and Botham remained from the previous season, and they were joined by Imran Khan, recovered from injury, Simon O'Donnell, Viv Richards and Graham Gooch. The last two could not be considered as top all-rounders, and O'Donnell's talent is still in embryo form, but Kapil Dev was away on Test duty and the competition was a good one.

This time each player faced twelve overs, two from each of his opponents. He began with a hundred points and lost 25 each time he was out. Naturally he added a run to his total every time he scored. The runs he conceded as a bowler were deducted from his total, and he earned 25 points for every wicket he took. The formula was repeated on the second day. Once again Rice was not out, and his 6 for 135 brought him to 243 which was again the winning total. He had proved a point. Len Owen, the organiser, suggested that he was the only one who had read the rules and really understood what had to be done to win. It is probably true, for he has never played a cricket match without thinking deeply and shaping his game accordingly.

Some suggested that the only real test of an all-rounder is how he performs over a season. Rice had been first in three seasons out of every four on that measure. Others suggested that an all-rounder can only be judged in the Test arena. When Kim Hughes brought his Australian rebels to South Africa in 1985–86 Rice proved his point there, for he led his team to victory and was named as his country's cricketer of the year. Where he has been given the opportunity, he has proved his worth.

He led Notts to the final of the Benson and Hedges Cup and to the NatWest Final. In 1984 they finished second to Essex in the county championship. Notts needed to beat Somerset on the last afternoon of the season, but they lost by 3 runs. Rice, with 3 sixes and 9 fours, hit 98 off 109 balls in a valiant attempt to win the match. He is never better than when the need is greatest. For three seasons he led Transvaal to total dominance in South African cricket.

He became an all-rounder 'because I always wanted to be in the game. I wanted to be doing something all the time. These days I try to provide a balance to whichever side I am playing for. Transvaal are strong in batting, but they need me as a bowler so I tend to emphasise that part of my game when I play for them. With Notts it has depended on whether or not Richard was playing, but generally I have felt my batting was needed in the middle order.'

Cricket has certainly needed him. He is a man of the utmost integrity, and his example as a cricketer and as a man is one which young players in the game would do well to follow.

If Rice has been denied the largest stage on which to act, although some would argue that the Australian side which Hughes took to South Africa was stronger than the one which Border brought to England, his friend and county colleague Richard Hadlee has had full scope to show his ability at the highest level.

He is the fourth son of Walter Hadlee, a good test batsman, a respected captain and an outstanding administrator. Two of Richard's four brothers played first-class cricket, and Dayle took 71 wickets for New Zealand. It was as a replacement for Dayle that Richard began his first-class career in January 1972. The elder brother could not play in Canterbury's last three matches in the Plunket Shield, and Richard, six months short of his 21st birthday, deputised. He hurled the ball down in his three matches and took 10 for 194. This was mainly as a result of a fine performance in the second innings of his last match of the season when he took 4 for 42. With the second ball of his eleventh over he had Ken Wadsworth leg before and followed this by bowling Furlong and Howell with his next two deliveries to complete the hat trick. It was an auspicious beginning.

His rise was rapid. In the 1972–73 season, he opened the Canterbury bowling with brother Dayle and took 30 wickets at 18·33 runs each. He had gained further experience with the New Zealand 'B' team in Australia, and in February 1973 he made his Test debut, against Pakistan in Wellington. He had Sadiq Mohammad caught, after he had scored 166, and caught and bowled Asif Iqbal, but his 18 overs conceded 84 runs. He was down at number nine, but Parker, who was also making his Test debut, broke a finger and did not bat. Richard Hadlee, his left-handed batting complementing his right-arm bowling, hit a brisk 46 in 49 minutes with 6 fours. He did not play again in the series, being replaced by brother Dayle, but he was in the party which came to England a few months later.

He played in only the first Test when the wicket of John Snow cost him 143 runs, but he was recognised as the most promising of the fast bowlers and performed particularly well late in the short tour to finish with 38 wickets. By his own admission, on that tour of England, Hadlee was wild and enthusiastic. He was a tearaway fast bowler whose main target seemed to be the middle of the pitch. As a batsman he was a slogger, and not a particularly successful one at that time. 'I was not an all-rounder at the beginning. I batted low in the order, and when you bat low down you do not take it seriously. You slog. It was only later, when I moved up to number six or five, that I began to develop concentration and feel that I was capable of building an innings as well as hitting hard.'

In Australia he showed that he had learned something from his experiences in England. He was still very expensive, but he had a good second Test in Sydney when he took 4 for 33 and 2 for 16. In the reciprocal Tests in New Zealand, he became a national hero for the first time. He took 3 for 59 in the first innings of the second Test and, vitally, bowled Walters with the first ball of the last over of the first day. Australia made 223, and New Zealand were 220 for 7 when Hadlee went in. He hit 23 and steered New Zealand to a 32-run lead. He then took 4 for 71, and with Glenn Turner making his second hundred of the match, New Zealand beat Australia for the first time.

This was the beginning of the greatest period in New Zealand cricket history, a foretaste of the glories that were to come. As yet Hadlee was not sure of a regular place in the New Zealand side, and he missed the first Test against India at Auckland in January 1976, but he was called up for the last two, and in the third, at Wellington, he took 4 for 35 and 7 for 23 to win the match. His last four wickets came in sixteen balls at the cost of three runs. His 11 for 58 established a New Zealand Test record which he was later to beat.

He was still a late order hard hitting batsman, but in the third Test in Karachi, October 1977, he and Warren Lees put on a record 186 in 179 minutes for New Zealand's seventh wicket. Hadlee hit what was then a career best 87, with 3 sixes and 6 fours, but he was aided by the fact that a frustrated Imran Khan had been banned from bowling by the umpire for bowling too many short pitched deliveries at Hadlee. Promoted to number seven, he hit 81 against Australia a few months later, but the significant thing about that Test in Auckland was that Dennis Lillee took his one hundred and fiftieth Test wicket.

Richard Hadlee is a serious man. He thinks, studies and works hard. He saw in Lillee a bowler on whom he chose to model himself, obtaining extra pace from a shorter run and an economy of effort. Rice, his captain at Nottinghamshire, appreciates the change that was brought about in Hadlee's bowling. 'His panther-like approach of fifteen paces makes his energy expenditure minimal and so his bowling spells can be longer. The batsmen suffer from a perpetual barrage of intelligent variations of pace and seam. He very seldom delivers the ball without having the seam perpendicular, and this feature of his bowling gives the ball the maximum chance of movement.'

The first country to feel the effect of the development in Hadlee's bowling was England at Basin Reserve, Wellington, in February 1978. In a low scoring match on a doubtful wicket, Hadlee scored a valuable 27 not out which had helped New Zealand to 228. He took the wickets of Randall, Roope, Botham and Old for 74 runs, and New Zealand took a first innings lead of 13. This hardly seemed significant when the home side were bowled out for 123 in their second innings so that England needed only 137 to win. They were out for 64. Hadlee took 6 for 26, bowling unchanged, and New Zealand beat England in a Test match for the first time.

Later that year he joined Nottinghamshire, and another period of his cricket education began. In his first three seasons for the county, the first of which coincided with the New Zealand tour of England in which he was engaged, he played only 23 games, took 96 wickets and scored 549 runs. For much of the time he was injured and unable to play. He was hesitant about renewing his contract after 1980, but encouraged by his wife Karen, a member of the New Zealand women's cricket team, and by Clive and Sue Rice, he set himself a programme of physical fitness and determined that he would prove to the English public his quality as a cricketer.

A season with Tasmania, 1979–80, convinced him further of the need to mould his approach to the wicket on the style of Lillee, to aim at greater economy while generating pace and movement. The placid wickets in Hobart, and elsewhere in Australia, were the graveyard of bowlers, but Hadlee learned there through hard work that wickets could still be taken on what were considered to be batsmen's paradises. He was to bring that learning to bear at Bath, Liverpool and elsewhere in England.

Geoff Howarth had taken over from Burgess as captain of New Zealand, and the promise that had been shown in the victories over Australia and England now came to fruition. In February 1980, the West Indies began a three-Test tour of New Zealand. The first Test was at Carisbrook, Dunedin. Clive Lloyd won the toss, and West Indies batted first. In Hadlee's second over, Greenidge was caught at square-leg when he unwisely attempted a hook. In his next over he trapped both Rowe and Kallicharran leg before. After half an hour West Indies were 4 for 3. Haynes made 55, but Hadlee finished with 5 for 34 and West Indies were all out for 140.

When Hadlee came to the wicket New Zealand were 159 for 6, and soon they were 168 for 7. He and Lance Cairns then added 54 in 36 minutes. Cairns made 30 and hit Parry for 3 sixes in an over. Parry did not bowl again in the series. Hadlee hit 9 fours and reached his fifty in 70 minutes. He was last out, caught at slip off Garner, and New Zealand led by 109. Haynes, who hit 105, and King were the only batsmen to withstand Hadlee in the second innings. He finished with 6 for 68, and when he caught and bowled Parry for his fifth wicket he had become the leading wicket-taker in New Zealand Test history.

New Zealand needed 104 to win. With the score on 44, Coney, Parker and Lees were all dismissed, and Webb went 10 runs later to make it 54 for 7. Hadlee hit 17, second top score, but was out at 73. Cairns stayed with Troup until the 100 was reached, and Troup and Boock got the last four runs, the winning one a leg-bye, to give New Zealand an historic victory by one wicket.

The West Indians did not take defeat well, and their truculence spilled over into the second Test which was drawn and in which the visitors behaved disgracefully. This petulant behaviour overshadowed Hadlee's first test century, 103, and the fact that, in his twenty-eighth Test match, he had become the first New Zealander to complete a thousand runs and take a hundred wickets in Test cricket.

New Zealand took the series, but a year later, in spite of some good all-round performances from Hadlee, they failed in Australia.

Hadlee returned to England for the 1981 season fitter and wiser. His only comment on the West Indian behaviour had been that he would have enjoyed his maiden Test century more if it had been made in a more friendly atmosphere, and his dignity and serious approach to the game were qualities which had won him admiration at Trent Bridge. Now they enthused over his bowling. In 1981 he took 105 wickets for Nottinghamshire and topped the national averages. He was the only bowler in the country to take a hundred wickets. He also scored 745 runs, including 142 not out against Yorkshire at Bradford. As we have said, Notts won the title by beating Glamorgan in the last match of the season at Trent Bridge. Rice won the toss and invited the Welshmen to bat. They were all out before lunch. Hadlee had taken 4 for 18 and reached his hundred wickets.

New Zealand's second victory over Australia, at Auckland, in March 1982, was a personal triumph for Hadlee who took 5 for 63 in the second innings, including a spell of 4 for 5, and, going in when two runs were needed, he hit Yardley for six. For Notts in 1982, he again performed with all-round brilliance. His 61 wickets put him top of the national averages, and he hit two centuries in his 807 runs. The county reached the Benson and Hedges final.

The claims of New Zealand in the World Cup and for their tour of England deprived Notts of his services for most of 1983. It was a season which, for Hadlee and for New Zealand, was one of muted joy. The Kiwis were strongly fancied to reach the final of the World Cup, but defeat by Sri Lanka meant that they were deprived of a place in the semi-final. They gained victory over England in a Test in England for the first

Richard Hadlee's success as an all-rounder of the very highest quality is the result of a natural ability enriched by determination and serious and consistent application.

time, but there was a strong feeling that they had not done themselves justice in the series.

'Chosen as man of the Series, Hadlee always lived up to his reputation and his own high standards. His bowling, off a shortened run-up, was a model for an aspiring fast bowler, full of variation, control and hostility. At 33 he remained one of the world's leading fast bowlers, as well as strengthening his claims to a place among the top all-rounders. His left-handed batting had few frills but his approach was undeniably effective. His 21 wickets were a record for a New Zealand bowler against England.'

What *Wisden* failed to mention was that when he bowled Cowans at Trent Bridge it was his two-hundredth wicket in Test cricket.

Whatever had been the disappointments of 1983, 1984 was to be a year of triumph. Willis took the England side to play three Tests in New Zealand, and the first, in Wellington, was drawn. The second encounter was at Lancaster Park, Christchurch, at the beginning of February. Howarth won the toss, but New Zealand slumped to 87 for 4, and 137 for 5, at which point Hadlee came in. He and Coney added 66 in 62 minutes, and he and Ian Smith put on 78 in 48 minutes. He reached fifty in 72 minutes off 47 balls, and when he was caught behind off Bob Willis for 99 he had faced only 81 balls, batted for 110 minutes and hit 18 fours. He then sent back Tavare, Gower and Randall for 16 runs, and when England followed on he took 5 for 28, and New Zealand won by an innings. They drew the third Test and so beat England in a series for the first time.

More records followed when Sri Lanka were beaten in Sri Lanka. In the three Tests Hadlee took 23 wickets at 10·75 runs each. Then he returned to England to resume his career with Nottinghamshire.

On 27 August 1984, at Trent Bridge, Richard Hadlee hit Chris Old of Warwickshire for four and completed a thousand runs for the season. As he had already taken more than a hundred wickets, he had become the first player to achieve the 'double' for seventeen years. Titmus had achieved the feat in 1967, but in 1969 the number of first-class fixtures in England had been reduced and since then the nearest anyone had come to the 'double' was the exciting West Indian Keith Boyce who played for Essex and took 82 wickets as well as scoring a thousand runs in 1972.

It should not be imagined that Hadlee's performance had come about by chance. He had dedicated himself to the idea and trained assiduously, pounding the streets in the early morning to ensure his fitness, and working hard in the gymnasium. His 117 wickets at 14·05 again placed him top of the bowling averages, while his 1,179 runs, average 51·26, placed him high in the batting.

The strength of the performance can be judged by reference to his innings of 210 not out against Middlesex at Lord's, the highest score of his career. Middlesex batted first, but lost two wickets, one to Hadlee, in the first nine balls of the match. Middlesex were bowled out for 152, Hadlee taking 4 for 55. Notts began dreadfully and were 17 for 4 when Hadlee joined Rice. He finished the day on 127 not out, having reached his hundred, against one of the strongest attacks in the country, off 93 balls. On the Monday, he nursed his partners and took Notts to 344. His 210 had come off 261 balls. Notts won by an innings after looking beaten on the Saturday afternoon.

What worlds were left to conquer? There remained two unscaled peaks, victory over Australia in a series and over England in a series in England. Both were to be accomplished within the space of a few months.

In November 1985, New Zealand began a three-match Test series against Australia. At Brisbane, Coney won the toss and asked Australia to bat. He was rewarded with instant success. The fifth ball of Hadlee's opening over was hooked by Hilditch to Chatfield at long leg who held the catch above his head. Boon and Wessels put on 69, but two overs before lunch Boon played back to Hadlee and was caught at slip. Hadlee's first ball after lunch was a wide half-volley which Border hit straight to Edgar at cover. Ten runs later Ritchie played back and was taken at slip by Martin Crowe. Wessels and Phillips battled on until bad light ended play early with Australia on 146 for 4.

Wessels was out to the fifth ball of the second morning when he offered no stroke to Hadlee and was leg before. It preluded a period of total disaster for Australia whose last 5 wickets fell for 29 runs in less than an hour. Four of these wickets went to Hadlee. The one wicket that was denied him in the innings was that of Lawson who looped an off-break from Vaughan Brown to mid-wicket where Hadlee himself took the catch. Hadlee's 9 for 52 was the fourth best bowling return in the history of Test cricket.

When New Zealand batted, Reid and Martin Crowe hit centuries, and Hadlee hit 4 sixes and 4 fours in a whirlwind 54. Australia were bowled out for 333 at their second attempt to give New Zealand victory by an innings. Hadlee took 6 for 71 to give him the best ever return by a New Zealander in Test cricket, and the eighth best in Test history. New Zealand won the third Test and the series, and Hadlee finished with an astounding record of 33 wickets in three Tests, five times in six innings he took 5 wickets or more.

Four months later Australia came to New Zealand, and again the

Kiwis, with Hadlee dominant, won the series. He took 16 wickets in the series, including 7 for 116 in the first innings of the second Test, and hit 72 not out in the first Test as he shared a seventh wicket stand of 132 with Jeremy Coney. Moreover, in that first Test, at Wellington, he claimed his three hundredth Test wicket when he had Border leg before. It was his sixty-first Test match. His last hundred wickets had come in seventeen matches.

In July 1986, New Zealand began their series against England with the better of a draw at Lord's. Hadlee took 6 for 80 and 1 for 78. It was appropriate that his great moment should come at Trent Bridge. Put in to bat, England were bowled out for 256. Hadlee took 6 for 80 and became third to Lillee and Botham as the greatest wicket-taker in Test cricket. At 144 for 5, New Zealand were struggling in reply, but Hadlee played his natural game and hit 68 while the resolute Evan Gray gave him fine support in a stand of 95. England had been blunted, and John Bracewell hit an excellent century to take his side to a first innings lead of 157. There was to be no respite from the menace of Hadlee. He took 4 for 60, and New Zealand went on to win by 8 wickets. The third Test at The Oval was marred by rain and was drawn so giving New Zealand their first series win in England.

It would be dangerous to believe that this was the summit of Hadlee's ambition although he finds the road-pounding and the preparation for a season less and less appealing. At the conclusion of the 1986 season, his benefit year, he was physically and mentally exhausted. But Clive Rice comments, 'When we think that there is nothing more for him to achieve in the game he will find some new milestone to reach or target to beat.'

He sets himself high standards and demands them from those around him, and he is as serious about a game for Canterbury or for Notts as he is about a Test match. It would be pleasant if that could be said about all those who play Test cricket. He stands with Botham as one who has scored two thousand runs and taken three hundred wickets in Test cricket, and he stands with Botham as one who has scored a thousand runs and taken a hundred wickets in limited-over internationals. When domestic figures are allied to those international facts, Richard Hadlee stands alone.

12

EASTERN STARS

One could argue that no cricket playing country has produced more all-rounders than India. The Indian team which beat England at Headingley in 1986 contained ten players who had scored centuries in first-class cricket, and it is not uncommon for India to field a side where all eleven players have scored hundreds. The most significant example of the worth of batsmen at numbers ten and eleven came when the Indian touring side of 1946 met Surrey at The Oval and Sarwate, number ten, scored 124 not out, while Bannerjee, number eleven, scored 121 in a last wicket stand of 249 which remains the highest made in England. Bannerjee did not play in a Test that summer, however, and Sarwate played only in one.

India's first Test captain, C. K. Nayudu, honoured by a statue in Indore, was an all-rounder of distinction in India, but he took only 9 wickets in his seven Test matches. India's two most noted all-rounders of the pre-partition period were Amar Singh and Amarnath, the father of Mohinder, a present stalwart of the national side.

Had he played Test cricket today, Ladha Amar Singh might well have established new records. As it was he was a highly successful Lancashire League player and his Test career was restricted to seven games against England between 1932 and 1936, but in his seven Tests he took 28 wickets with his right-arm fast-medium and hit some brisk runs. He was highly regarded by the England batsmen who were disconcerted by his pace off the pitch. He sent back 7 for 86 at Madras in 1934 and shattered England at Lord's in 1936 with 6 for 35 which remains a record for India in England. More remarkably, as a batsman he hit 131 not out against Lancashire at Blackpool in 1932 when going in at number ten.

It was intended that Amar Singh's main support on the 1936 tour should be Lala Amarnath, and in the run-up to the first Test Amarnath was outstanding, scoring 613 runs and taking 32 wickets. But the Indian team was torn apart by internal divisions, and Amarnath was sent home as a disciplinary measure before the Test series began. He was later exonerated and was to return to England in 1946 and to captain India in Australia.

An exciting romantic figure, Lala Amarnath played his cricket with panache. He bowled medium pace from a short, easy run, and he batted with an ebullience. He was the first Indian to score a century in a Test match, at Bombay in 1933. He captained India in their first series against Pakistan, 1952–53, so that his twenty-four Tests spanned twenty years, but by then India had found a truly great all-rounder, Mulwantrai Himmatlal Mankad, known better as 'Vinoo' Mankad.

Mankad was known at home by his pet name of 'Minu', but his schoolfriends converted this into 'Vinoo'. The name stuck, and, in later life, even the name plate on the door of his flat in Bombay read 'Vinoo Mankad'. His elder son, Ashok, who was to play Test cricket, took the name 'Vinoo' for himself.

Mankad's father was a doctor in government service and had to travel widely so that the boy was brought up by an uncle. The uncle encouraged him to play cricket, and his school, Nawanagar High School, played no other game. He was picked out by the school coach, Indian Test cricketer Sorabji Colah, as an outstanding prospect. Cricket so dominated his time that his education was to remain incomplete as he was playing against Lord Tennyson's team in 1937–38 at the time when he should have been taking examinations.

Mankad thrived in schools cricket, and from 1935 to 1940 he was coached by Albert Wensley, the Sussex all-rounder who had done the 'double' in 1929. Wensley was a tremendous influence on the young Mankad who, from an early age, threw the ball faster with his left hand than his right even though he batted right-handed. He took to bowling left-arm medium pace, but Wensley persuaded him to bowl slow spin. The old Sussex professional taught him the art of flight, variation of spin and advised him to disregard off-breaks in fear that they would cause him to lose his natural grip and action for the slow left-armer's natural leg-break. Following Wensley's advice, Mankad bowled slow left-arm for months' practice at a stretch, going without batting at all during this period. Such painstaking devotion was to be characteristic of Mankad throughout his life.

In batting, Wensley allowed Mankad to take no undue risks, encouraging him to build a big score without frills. In 1936, Nawanagar, on the west coast of India midway between Bombay and Karachi, formed its own cricket team, and at the insistence of Duleepsinhji, one of the legendary figures in Indian cricket though his Test matches, like those of his uncle

'Ranji', were played for England, Mankad was picked to open the innings. He was not an immediate success, showing a fallibility on leg stump, but Duleepsinhji organised special practice under his guidance and moulded Mankad into an opener.

In November 1935, at the age of 18, Mankad made his first-class debut, for Western India States against Jack Ryder's Australians at Rajkot. A month later he made his debut in the Ranji Trophy, playing for Western India States against Bombay at Poona. Two years later he scored his first century in first-class cricket and was picked to play in the second of the representative matches against Lionel Tennyson's side. He hit 38 and 88 and sent back Wellard and Tennyson for six runs in his two overs. In the next match, in Calcutta, he took 4 for 47 and bowled India to victory.

The England cricketers noted him as a player of outstanding quality, and Pelham Warner, writing in *The Cricketer*, spoke of him as 'an exceptionally good all-round cricketer. He rarely, if ever, failed as a batsman against the tourists, was a remarkably accurate left-hand bowler and the manner in which he caught Edrich at short-leg in the Test at Calcutta was an astounding effort.'

England were scheduled to play a Test series in India in 1939–40, but the war caused its cancellation so that Mankad's entry into Test cricket was delayed seven years. No other great all-rounder suffered such a setback to his career.

The 1946 tour of England by the Indian side was the last before partition. Captained by the Nawab of Pataudi, India lost the first Test and drew the other two. Mankad's Test career began with innings of 14 and 63, top score for India in the match, and 2 for 107 in 48 overs. He also pulled off a magnificent catch at short fine-leg to dismiss Washbrook. He was the outstanding cricketer of the tour. He scored 1,120 runs and took 129 wickets so becoming the first Indian to complete the 'double' and the last touring player to achieve the feat in England. It is highly unlikely that either of these records will be beaten.

C. B. Fry thought him the best left-arm spinner in the world, and *Wisden* named him as one of the five cricketers of the year. Pataudi gave him no settled place in the batting order, and he hovered between number one and number seven, but he brought to all that he did an uncomplaining gaiety.

Only two Indians, Amar Singh and Amarnath, had played in the northern leagues before the war, but Mankad's form on the 1946 tour drew the attention of many clubs. He accepted an offer from the Central Lancashire League side Castleton Moor, but, because of family reasons, he was unable to play for them until 1948. In his first year in the League he completed the 'double', a remarkable achievement.

He played for Castleton Moor until 1951, and later played for Haslingden, Stockport and Tonge. He played in the Leagues for fifteen consecutive seasons, which is a world record, and his experiences there had a significant effect upon his approach to the game. In 1946 he was a batsman of impregnable defence, but limited in strokes. When he next played against England he could hit all round the wicket.

At Test level, his batting had shown an extra dimension in the series in Australia, 1947–48. He hit India's first century in a Test match against Australia, at Melbourne, and followed this with another on the same ground in the fifth Test. He scored 889 runs on the tour and took 61 wickets, twice as many as any other bowler, and once again he did a vast amount of work. On the eve of the team's departure for India, Don Bradman, who had gone to the airport to see the visitors off, handed Mankad an envelope. Inside was a signed photograph with the inscription 'Well bowled, Mankad'. The all-rounder considered that it was the most important of all the tributes paid to him during his career.

India engaged in a home series against West Indies the following year, and when one comes to assess the magnitude of Mankad's achievement in Test cricket one needs to reflect on the amount of work that he was asked to do on wickets which were batsmen's paradises. In the first Test he bowled 59 overs and took 2 for 176 as the West Indians reached 631, and in the second Test he took 3 for 202 in 75 overs as they scored 629 for 6 declared. He had still to play in a winning side in a Test match.

The season 1951–52 was a memorable one in Mankad's career, just as it was memorable for India. Mankad switched to Bombay and hit 141 in the Ranji Trophy Final which his side won. The England side under Nigel Howard were India's Test opponents, and for Mankad the series was a triumph. England won the fourth Test, but India won the fifth Test to level the rubber. It was India's twenty-fifth Test match and her first victory.

Having batted number ten and number nine in the second Test, Mankad opened with Pankaj Roy in the third Test and scored 59 and 71 not out in a stand of 103, the only century opening stand for India in the series. The great triumph came at Madras, however, when England were bowled out for 266 and 183. Mankad took 8 for 55 and 4 for 53, an innings analysis and match analysis which remain records for India against England. India won by an innings and Mankad finished the series with 34 wickets at 16·97 apiece, and this 'on pitches seldom suitable to him'.

It seems incredible to look back more than thirty years and find that the Indian Board would not guarantee Mankad a place in the party of seventeen to tour England a few months after his successes against Howard's team. He had been offered a contract by Haslingden which was lucrative, and he asked the Board if he would be in the side to come to England. They refused to answer him, and he had no option but to sign for the Lancashire League club. The Board felt that they could not set a precedent by assuring a player of his place in advance of the others, and then they added a worse insult by being quoted in *The Times of India* as saying that Mankad's services would not be utilised in the four Tests in England even if he were made available. For one who was such an unquestioning team-man, this was shabby treatment.

On the eve of the first Test at Headingley, the Indian manager and the captain, Hazare, cabled the Board for permission to play Mankad as they were bedevilled by injury and inexperience. The permission was given and Mankad arrived at the team hotel, but the Board then failed to agree terms with Haslingden and he did not play. India, 0 for 4 in the second innings, lost by seven wickets.

The touring side was in a sorry plight, and agreement was reached that enabled Mankad to play in the three remaining Tests. India lost the series quite disastrously, but the eight-wicket defeat at Lord's became known as Mankad's Test. He and Pankaj Roy began the match with a stand of 106 which ended twenty minutes after lunch when Mankad was brilliantly caught by Watkins for 72. India then collapsed to be all out for 235. Hutton and Evans hit centuries for England who reached 537. Mankad sent down 73 overs and took 5 for 196.

India wanted 302 to avoid the innings defeat when they went in again at 3.45 p.m. Although Mankad had bowled 31 of his overs that day, he not only opened once more but batted even better than on the first day. The loss of Roy and Adhikari at 59 did not deter him. He pulled the first ball from Jenkins for 6 and with Hazare raised the score to 137 for two wickets at the close.

On the fourth day, Mankad and Hazare took their partnership to 211. Mankad attacked the bowling in an exciting manner. Trueman, with new ball, rapped him painfully on the fingers. He responded by taking 17 off Trueman's next over. Fifteen minutes after lunch, overtaken by fatigue, he was yorked by Laker. In four and a half hours he had hit 184, with a six and 19 fours. It was, at the time, the highest score made for India in a Test match.

When he was out India were 270 for 3. They were all out for 308. He then bowled another 24 overs and conceded only 35 runs as England moved to victory.

The English press was unanimous in its praise, ranking him with Miller as the world's leading all-rounder. *The Times* stated, 'Mankad's performance in this match has been something to remember for a long time. For endurance and skill it has possessed all the breadth of the plains of his homeland and all the heights of the Himalayas.'

The return to India heralded an historic occasion. At Delhi, on 16 October 1952, Pakistan entered Test cricket. The celebration was to belong to Mankad rather than to Pakistan. India won the first Test by an innings and 70 runs. Mankad returned figures of 8 for 52 and 5 for 79 which established new records for India.

He had been troubled in that Test by a sore spinning finger which kept him out of the next match, which Pakistan won, but he returned for the third Test. This was played at Bombay, and Mankad took 3 for 52 and 5 for 72, and scored 41 and 35 not out. It was his twenty-third Test match, and when, in the second innings, Waqar Hassan was caught at short-leg by Hazare off Mankad it gave the all-rounder his hundredth wicket in Test cricket and thereby the 'double'. At that time, no player had reached a thousand runs and a hundred wickets in Test cricket in fewer Tests, and his record was to stand until 1979 when Botham reached the mark in his twenty-first Test.

Not only did Mankad produce another match-winning all-round performance in that Test, but he also gave another display of incredible stamina. His second innings analysis was 65 overs, 31 maidens, 72 runs, and 5 wickets, and he followed this by going out to open the innings, hitting 35 out of 45 and square cutting Fazal Mahmood for the winning hit.

He was vice-captain of the Indian side in the West Indies 1952–53 where he again bowled mammoth stints and he captained India in Pakistan 1954–55. All five Tests were drawn and he failed to bring to his leadership the qualities which made him so renowned as a cricketer.

When Cave brought the New Zealand side to India for the first Test series between the two countries, 1955–56, Mankad was replaced as captain by Umrigar. The change had a beneficial effect upon his cricket. In the first Test, Umrigar hit 223, India's first double century in Test cricket. Mankad reached exactly the same score in the second Test and bettered it with an innings of 231 in the fifth Test, at Madras. He and Pankaj Roy set up a world record for Test cricket with an opening stand of 413 in 472 minutes. Mankad was caught on the boundary trying to hit

Moir out of the ground. Not only was it the highest Test innings for India at the time, but it also took Mankad past the two thousand run mark in Test cricket. For good measure he finished off the New Zealanders in their second innings with 4 for 65.

That was the high peak of his Test career. From that point he went into decline. He took 4 for 49 in Australia's last Test with Johnson as captain, and that was his last creditable performance in a Test match. When Alexander came with the West Indian side of 1958–59, Mankad was already past his prime. He was selected for the fourth and fifth Tests, and in the fourth Test found himself as captain when Umrigar resigned after a disagreement with the Board shortly before the match. He bowled well, while the West Indies scored 500, and his 4 for 95 came from 38 overs. Gilchrist bowled him for 4, and on the fourth day he developed a swelling on his arm which prevented him from taking any further part in the match.

He played in the fifth Test in Delhi, but on a lifeless pitch he could do nothing and his 55 overs cost him 167 runs without reward. He hit a brisk 21 in the first innings, and then in the second he was bowled between bat and pad by Collie Smith for 0. An off-break bowler would not have done that four years earlier. He was not selected for a Test match again. He was 42. He played cricket for another three years, but the glory was gone.

His contribution to Indian cricket was immeasurable. He had played in some of the country's weaker sides and had, at times, been virtually unsupported in his efforts. His stamina was one of the finest of his qualities. He exercised regularly, practised consistently, dieted carefully, observed strict hours, and played continuously. He was patient and daring. He was modest and cheerful, and he possessed a big heart and a cool head.

He died on 21 April 1978, and six months later the man who was to challenge him for the title of India's greatest all-round cricketer made his Test debut.

Ramlal Nikhanj Kapil Dev made no great impression in his first Test series which was against Pakistan except to suggest that India had at last found what she most desired, a fast bowler. It was also obvious that he was a very clean and hard striker of the ball as he proved with a violent 59 in the third Test.

Within weeks of the series in Pakistan India were entertaining West Indies, who were weakened by the absence of their Packer players. In the third Test, Kapil Dev hit 61, and he followed this with 4 for 38 and 3 for 46 as India won by three wickets. The fifth Test saw him reach a maiden

Test century, and his 126 not out came off only 124 balls. He hit 11 fours and a six. The six was off Norbert Phillip and it brought Kapil Dev to three figures. India won the series; Kapil Dev scored 62 in the last Test, and a star was born.

His rapid rise to international fame came as no surprise to the followers of the game in India. Coached by Desh Prem Azad, Kapil Dev was an outstanding schoolboy cricketer. He was a few weeks short of his 17th birthday when he made his first-class debut in 1975. Two years later, in an inter-university non-first-class match, he scored 327 for Punjab University against Hissar Agriculture University. More importantly, in a country where great spinners had thrived, there was a paucity of pace bowlers, and Kapil Dev emerged from the north as the answer to a prayer, a strike bowler, strong, quick and able to move the ball.

His arrival in England in 1979 was awaited with interest. He made little impact in the Prudential World Cup in which India had a miserable time culminating in defeat by Sri Lanka. However, by then Kapil Dev had already made his mark with 102 in 74 minutes against Northamptonshire in the opening match of the Indian tour. A phenomenal amount of work fell upon him. He bowled 48 overs and took 5 for 146 in the first Test at Lord's, and captured wickets regularly in the series.

Test matches spilled one upon another in the next few months. On their return from England, India played a six-match series against Australia and won. Kapil hit a blistering 83 in the first Test, but it was as a bowler that his greatest success came. In the third Test, Australia, needing 279 in 312 minutes, looked set to win, but Kapil Dev broke their innings and, ably suported by Shivlal Yadav, bowled them out for 125. Five wickets in the first innings of the fourth Test and five in the first innings of the fifth were followed by triumph in the sixth Test when his 4 for 39 in the second innings brought India victory and a win in a rubber against Australia for the first time.

A fortnight later, the first Test against Pakistan began. His run of success continued unabated, and when he took 6 for 63 in the fourth Test which ended on 29 December (there was no play on the last scheduled day) he brought his total of Test wickets for 1979 to a world record 74. He had appeared in seventeen Test matches in the year.

The sixth Test, completed on 3 February 1980, was drawn, but by then India had won the series. It was a momentous occasion for Kapil Dev. He took his hundredth Test wicket and two days later hit his thousandth Test run. It was his twenty-fifth Test in succession, and in completing the 'double' he had taken only 1 year, 105 days, a record. He was 21 years, 25

Kapil Dev – a man of fun and joy who has led India to her greatest triumphs.

days old when he took his hundredth wicket, the youngest player to achieve this in Test cricket, and he was also the youngest player to reach a thousand runs as well as being the youngest to record the 'double'. As he had been asked to play a Test match every three weeks on average since his debut, and in his fifteen months of international cricket had also included a world cup, a tour to England and three one-day internationals, he had shown an amazing record of consistency, fitness and stamina. The proliferation in Test cricket had given him the opportunity to set records quickly, but he had responded with 28 wickets at 22·35 runs each against Australia and 32 at 17·68 against Pakistan, as well as producing some furious batting achievements.

Glories tumbled over each other in the next three years. He had a highly successful tour as a bowler in Australia. He hit a hundred off 84 balls in the series in which India beat England in India and followed this with a memorable 97 off 93 balls when India were struggling at The Oval. As India fell to Pakistan he became the first bowler to concede two hundred runs in an innings against Pakistan, but his figures were 7 for 220, and two Tests later he took 8 for 85.

He was named as India's captain for the tour to the West Indies in 1983, and celebrated by reaching two thousand runs in Test cricket in his first match as captain. In the next Test, his fiftieth, he became the youngest player to reach two hundred wickets in Test cricket. He was 24 years, 67 days old.

From the West Indies, India came to England for the third World Cup. Nobody considered that they had any chance of winning the trophy, and the bookmakers quoted odds of 60 to 1 against them. There was a surprising win over West Indies in the opening game which stimulated interest, but defeat by Australia at Trent Bridge and a further reverse in the return match against West Indies seemed to set the pattern of predictability. Zimbabwe had been beaten once, but India were scheduled to meet them again at Tunbridge Wells.

There can be few lovelier cricket grounds in the world than the Nevil Ground, enclosed by trees and, in high summer, banked by rhododendrons, but it seemed an unlikely venue for India and Zimbabwe. Kapil Dev won the toss and chose to bat. It was a bright morning with a slight breeze. For India, the start was disastrous.

Gavaskar was leg before to the last ball of the opening over. Scoring was limited to a leg-bye, a single and a four when, in the fifth over, Amarnath was caught behind. Immediately Srikkanth hit high and wild to deep mid-off. Patil was caught behind down the leg side, and Yashpal

Sharma also gave a catch to the wicket-keeper. After 13 overs, India were 17 for 5.

Kapil Dev had come to the wicket at 11.25 a.m. with the score at 9 for 4. From the start he was purposeful. He combined watchful defence with an eagerness to hit the ball, but there was no hint of rashness, nor any sign of lapse in concentration. He and Binny offered India some relief in a stand of 60, but Traicos frustrated Binny and had him leg before, and Shastri played wildly to be caught at mid-off, 78 for 7. Madan Lal played sensibly and busily, and in the thirty-sixth over Kapil Dev raised his fifty and India's hundred. At lunch, India had reached 106.

It was the period immediately after lunch in which Kapil Dev stamped his authority on the game. He took 12 runs in an over from Rawson, and he and Madan Lal added 62 in 16 overs before Madan Lal was caught behind, 140 for 8. Syed Kirmani joined Kapil Dev.

Never at any time did Kapil Dev violate a sound technique as, with maturity and composure, he began to hit the ball to all parts of the ground. In 13 thrilling overs, he and Kirmani added 100 runs. When Kapil Dev hit in the air it was to send the ball cascading to the boundary. He played an innings of supreme majesty and power. He reached his century in the forty-ninth over, and in the last eleven overs of the innings he scored at the rate of seven an over. He hit 6 sixes and 16 fours and his 175 not out spanned 50 overs. He came in at 9 for 4, and India ended at 266 for 8. Then he opened the bowling and India won the match by 31 runs.

Two days later, they beat Australia at Chelmsford with ease. At Old Trafford, they swept England aside in the semi-final, and a week after facing defeat by Zimbabwe at Tunbridge Wells India triumphed over West Indies at Lord's, and Kapil Dev, a national hero, was holding aloft the World Cup.

There was something of a reaction in the months that followed, and Kapil Dev was deprived of the captaincy. However, Gavaskar fared little better, and Kapil Dev was reinstated.

A more positive approach might well have brought India victory over Australia in 1985–86, but Kapil Dev had the consolation of reaching three thousand runs in Test cricket. He was chosen to lead the side to England although, in twenty Tests as captain, he had not won a match.

Kapil Dev is a joyous person. He is always ready to break into a smile or a laugh. Fun bubbles in the man, and it bubbles in his cricket, but, until 1986, it had not bubbled in his captaincy except in the one-day game. In 1986 he came to England with a single purpose, to entertain, but the capacity to entertain was now tinged with the wisdom and experience gained from 74 Test matches. His field placings and bowling changes were masterful. His zest for the game carried his side with him. England were outplayed in batting, bowling and fielding. It was not simply a triumph for India, it was a joy for cricket.

The Indian captain's own contribution was immeasurable. In the second innings of the first Test at Lord's, he dismissed Gooch, Robinson and Gower in the space of nineteen deliveries, and when India, needing 134 to win, were 78 for 5 he hit a hurricane 23 and finished the match by pulling Edmonds into the Grandstand Balcony. In the decisive win at Headingley, he hit another ferocious 31 when it was desperately needed and sent back Gooch with only 12 on the board.

He and his team returned home as heroes and played a tied Test with Australia, a wonderful game which another captain would have condemned to a draw on the last day. Kapil Dev hit his fourth Test hundred, and in the 1986–87 series against Sri Lanka equalled Botham's record of three thousand runs and three hundred wickets in Test cricket.

The major factor in assessing Kapil Dev's massive achievement is that for much of his career he has had the disadvantage of not having a strike bowler along with him so that the pressure has been entirely on him. Opponents have known that they need only to survive against him to thrive against the other bowlers. In batting, his natural game has continued to flow in spite of once being dropped for a rash shot. Perhaps most importantly, he has set an example in bowling and batting which aspiring young players in India are trying to follow.

It is interesting to note that Kapil Dev was born in Chandigarh on 6 January 1959, and that his parents came from what is now Pakistan, but they emigrated from their home near Rawalpindi at the time of partition. If they had not, Kapil Dev could well have been opening the bowling for Pakistan with Imran Khan, his rival for the title of greatest all-rounder on the Indian subcontinent.

Pakistan's entry into Test cricket came in October 1952, more than five years after partition. Their first victory came as early as August 1954, when England were beaten at The Oval.

As with India, Pakistan fielded sides where the majority were capable batsmen, but in March 1959 Mushtaq Mohammad made his debut at the age of 15 years, 124 days. A member of a famous cricketing family, Mushtaq was to score 3,643 runs and take 79 wickets in Test cricket. He was also to perform admirably for Northamptonshire for some years. An attractive, cultured, aggressive right-handed batsman, Mushtaq bowled leg-breaks and googlies, but his bowling was to be required less and less, particularly after the advent of Intikhab Alam.

Mushtaq scored two Test centuries before he was 19 years old. He was a cricketer of finesse rather than force, and although he was aggressive by nature, he had great powers of concentration like his brother Hanif. As a bowler, he had control and the ability to spin the ball appreciably and his Test record is a good one, but it is unlikely that he would have been selected for Pakistan purely as a bowler.

Intikhab, on the other hand, was primarily a bowler, although as an aggressive batsman he gave delight to supporters of both Pakistan and Surrey, and he was the first Pakistani to acheive the 'double' in Test cricket. He was the captain of Pakistan when they won their first Test series overseas, against New Zealand, 1972–73, but above all he was a cheerful cricketer who gave fun wherever he went. That good humour has helped him to become a most popular and successful manager of touring sides.

He was among the top flight of leg-break and googly bowlers, and a burly, late order hard-hitting batsman, relying mainly on driving off the front foot. With his first ball in Test cricket he bowled Colin McDonald, the Australian opener, but it was some years before he was to have consistent success. His one Test century came when he and Mushtaq put on 145 for Pakistan's sixth wicket against England at Hyderabad in 1973. Intikhab hit 138 which included 4 sixes and 15 fours. A year later, in his forty-first Test, he bowled Alan Knott at The Oval and completed the 'double'. By then, Imran Khan was a regular member of the Pakistan side, and with more than two thousand runs and two hundred Test wickets to his credit, he is unquestionably the one Pakistan cricketer who would have been picked for the team as both a batsman and a bowler. Indeed, for a period when his injured leg prevented him from bowling, he captained the side purely as a batsman.

Before the shin stress fracture which hampered him for more than a year, Imran Khan was as fast as any bowler in the world. He was also a gloriously attacking batsman, and once he became captain of Pakistan he added a sense of responsibility. He is still among the most penetrating of fast bowlers and entertaining of batsmen although some of his county colleagues would suggest that his bowling has lost a fraction of its edge.

He has always been surrounded by an aura of charm, aristocracy and controversy. He is a glamorous public figure, but he is also one who has roused passions of antagonism, and in Pakistan his reputation rose to supreme heights, plummeted and now has risen again.

Imran Khan Niazi was born in Lahore of a wealthy family. Javed Burki and Majid Khan, both Pakistan Test players, are his cousins. In 1971, at the age of 18, he was chosen for Pakistan's tour of England. He played only in the first Test, was run out for 5 and failed to take a wicket. He was thin, had an unruly mop of hair and bowled short, fast and wild. He played for Worcestershire second team, hit a century and took 13 expensive wickets. In his appearance for Worcestershire against the other tourists that season, India, he was massacred by Gavaskar and Wadekar.

Following the 1971 season, he completed his education at Worcester Royal Grammar School, and, in 1973, he went up to Keble College, Oxford. He was in the University side all three years, and he was captain in 1974 when, following the University match, he joined the Pakistan touring side. He played in all three Tests, took his first Test wicket, Greig, but accomplished little. What was apparent, however, was that he had developed physically, that he possessed a magnificent athletic body, that his batting had improved considerably and that he was quick and could bowl a fearsome bouncer.

He came down from Oxford in 1975 and played for Worcestershire in 1976. He 'fulfilled the county's hopes that he could develop as the natural successor to d'Oliveira. By scoring a century and taking thirteen wickets in an innings victory over Lancashire, he was identified as an all-rounder of world-class possibilities. In all, he scored four Championship hundreds, including an unforgettable 166 when running out of partners at Northampton, while his hostile new-ball bowling, with massive in-swing, placed him on top of the county's bowling averages with 65 wickets.'

That was to be Imran's last season with Worcestershire. In 1977 he announced that he was moving to Sussex. Worcestershire had given him much help in his education and in his formative years as a cricketer, and there was anger and dismay at his move. Imran received a three-month suspension, and the rift with Worcestershire has never been truly healed in many people's minds. When, in 1986, he routed the Worcestershire middle order in the semi-final of the NatWest Bank Trophy at New Road, he was the victim of much abuse. It was interpreted as racist in most quarters, but it had its basis in his departure from the county in 1977. The reasons that he offered later were that he found the life in Worcester frustratingly parochial and provincial, and that he was essentially urban and wished to live in the south in easy reach of London.

He worked hard to add the out-swinger to his bowling armoury, and he became a number five batsman of dashing strokes. At Test level, he

Imran Khan. Penetrating fast bowler, attacking batsman, serious student of the game and imperious captain.

began to thrive, and when Pakistan beat Australia in Australia for the first time, in January 1977, he had match figures of 12 for 165.

He followed this with an excellent series in the West Indies, but then came Packer and divided loyalties. Imran asserts that it was what he learned in World Series Cricket that made him one of the game's great fast bowlers. Both Procter and Snow advised him on run-up and delivery, and his technical competence as a bowler increased.

At Lahore, the town of his birth, on his 28th birthday, 25 November 1980, he hit his first Test century, for Pakistan against West Indies, and when he had scored 21 he became the second Pakistani to complete the 'double' in Test cricket. It was his thirtieth Test.

In 1981–82, he was named as the player of the series when Pakistan lost two Tests to one in Australia and he became Pakistan's leading wicket-taker in Test cricket, but controversy followed this tour as the leading players, Imran foremost amongst them, rebelled against the captaincy of Javed Miandad. They refused to play under his leadership unless a new captain was named for the forthcoming tour to England. The Board of Pakistan stood firm, and several leading players did not make themselves available for the first two Tests against Sri Lanka in March 1982. Javed decided to relinquish the captaincy of the team to tour England, and the players returned for the third and final Test. Imran took 8 for 58 and 6 for 58, and Pakistan won by an innings. He became the first Pakistan bowler to take 14 wickets in a Test and the first to reach 150 wickets in Test cricket. He was named as captain for the side to tour England.

His captaincy was outstanding although not without controversy, and his own contribution to the series, which Pakistan rather unluckily lost by two to one, was magnificent. He had match figures of 9 for 136 and played a brave innings of 65 in the first Test, led his side to a memorable victory at Lord's and took 8 wickets and scored 67 and 46 at Headingley. His batting had grown in maturity. He was a responsible and passionate leader. His bitter disappointment at Pakistan's failure to win the series was apparent to all.

Now a period of great prosperity for Pakistan cricket began. He led them to a triumph over Australia when they won all three Tests of the series. This was followed by the destruction of India. At Karachi, he took 3 for 19 and 8 for 60. In the next Test, at Faisalabad, he took 6 for 98 and 5 for 82, and he hit 117 off 121 balls. He took 21 off one over from Kapil Dev, and, in all, he hit 5 sixes and 10 fours. Pakistan won by an innings, as they did the next Test when he took 8 for 80 in the match. He finished the series with 40 wickets at 13·95 runs each. *Wisden* called his 53 wickets in nine Test matches on Pakistan pitches, always detrimental to the bowler, the outstanding individual performance of the year.

This was the pinnacle of achievement. He suffered a stress fracture of the shin and was unable to bowl. There were high hopes of Pakistan success in the World Cup, but, although they rather fortunately reached the semi-final, with Imran unable to bowl they were a pale imitation of the side that had trounced India and Australia.

Following the World Cup, he scored consistently for Sussex when he would have been better advised to rest. He bowled only 46·2 overs at less than half pace, but remarkably, at Edgbaston, he took 6 for 6 including the hat trick.

In Pakistan, criticism of him mounted. He was not in the side that went to Australia. He was held responsible for Pakistan's failure in the World Cup. It was said that he had shown too much favouritism to Abdul Qadir and Mansoor Akhtar in his reign as captain, and that the claims of Qasim Umar had been ignored. In England, his social life was accorded almost as many words of print by the tabloid press as were the doings of Ian Botham.

Imran had appeared little in domestic cricket in Pakistan and was critical of the structure. The lot of a captain of Pakistan is never an easy one, and even on the eve of the 1986–87 series against West Indies, one of the leading cricket journalists of the country could write: 'The question, however, is: can all concerned rise above the self and play for their country instead of playing for themselves and against each other.' By 1984, Imran Khan, the most successful captain, bowler and all-rounder that Pakistan has ever produced, had fallen from favour. He was a prophet unrecognised in his own country. He chose to play for New South Wales in Australia in 1984–85.

It was a very wise decision. He was able to recuperate from his serious injury and to nurse himself back to top speed gradually. By the time the Sheffield Shield Final arrived he was at his best and took 9 for 100 in the match against Queensland. New South Wales swept the board in Australia and Imran finished top of the Australian bowling averages.

Meanwhile, the Pakistan side had been suffering in New Zealand. They had been beaten in the Tests and the one-day series, and Abdul Qadir had been sent home as a disciplinary measure. His 'crime' was never fully explained, and he was later exonerated. When Pakistan went to Australia for the Benson and Hedges World Championship of Cricket, which commemorated the one hundred and fiftieth anniversary of the founding of the state of Victoria, Imran was asked to join the side. Pakistan reached the final.

He was retained when West Indies played a one-day series in Pakistan, and he topped the bowling averages in the three-match Test series against Sri Lanka a few weeks later. At the end of the series, Javed Miandad again stood down as captain. Imran was asked to lead the side to Sri Lanka in February 1986. The rehabilitation was complete.

As the West Indies prepared to do battle in Pakistan at the end of 1986, Imran Khan could look back on 58 Tests which had brought him 2,140 runs and 264 wickets. He stands head and shoulders above all other cricketers of Pakistan. In world cricket today, he vies with Kapil Dev, Richard Hadlee and Ian Botham for the title of 'the greatest all-rounder'.

13

BOTH!

Inevitably, the name of Ian Terence Botham has intruded upon this narrative. He is not a man whom it has been possible to keep out of the news since he entered cricket in 1974. He is a big man in all that he does, and, like all the greatest of all-round cricketers from W.G. Grace onwards, he demands a response. So large is he in conception and performance that when, in the Texaco Trophy match at Old Trafford in 1985, he hit the top score of 72 and was bowled by Greg Matthews as he attempted a reverse sweep, he received only criticism for getting out in such a manner and was blamed for England's defeat. His colleagues, Gower and Lamb, scored 3 and 0.

He is a physical cricketer. The emphasis of his game is on force and power, not on finesse. Even those breathtaking slip catches are displays of masculine prowess, chest-beating examples of his joy in his ability. His batting is a thing of might. One never remembers a Botham innings for the subtlety of shot or the patience of accumulation; one remembers it for the tremendous free swing of the bat on the off or cover drive, or for the violent and spectacular hook shots. He has an unquenchable delight in the game, and his every movement on a cricket field says 'watch me'. No cricketer since W.G. Grace has been so supremely confident of his own ability, and when, as it must, that ability fails him on rare occasions, he is naïvely bewildered and sees in press or authority the giants that Don Quixote saw in windmills.

He was born in Heswall in Cheshire in 1955, but when his father retired from the Fleet Air Arm in 1958 the family moved to Yeovil where Leslie Botham had got a job with Westland Helicopters which, some years later, for a brief period of time, were to become almost as famous as Botham himself.

Ian Botham had a passion for cricket and a natural ability that was obvious to all observers of the game. What was also obvious was that his way of doing things was entirely his own. He played for the Somerset youth side under the guidance of Bill Andrews, a fine county all-rounder of the 1930s and a man of infinite zest and humour, spent some time on the ground staff at Lord's and played two John Player League games at the end of the 1973 season. The following year, when Cartwright was injured, he played in the county championship.

His impact on the first-class game was promising rather than dramatic. It was felt that he showed 'star quality'. 'His lively right-arm swing bowling, clean flowing driving, and the ability to field anywhere were soon evident.' His great moment came in the quarter-final of the Benson and Hedges Cup against Hampshire at Taunton.

Hampshire were bowled out for 182, Botham taking the all-important wicket of Barry Richards and later capturing Peter Sainsbury. Somerset slumped to 113 for 8 and looked well beaten. Botham, at number nine, found a gallant partner in Moseley, and they added 63 in 13 overs. Botham was hit in the mouth by a bouncer from Andy Roberts, but, having spat out two teeth, he continued. Clapp saw that he kept the bowling, and when the penultimate over arrived Somerset needed three to win. Herman three times beat Botham, but the last ball of the over was hammered through the covers for a Somerset victory. The young man was cheered from the field. He had made 45 not out and won the Gold Award. Not for the last time he was the hero of a cricket match.

In the next couple of years he grew in strength. His captain, Brian Close, suggested that he might end his career exclusively as a batsman. He responded by taking a hundred wickets in 1978, but by then he was an England player.

In 1976, he hit his maiden first-class hundred, was capped by Somerset, for whom he scored 944 runs and took 60 wickets, and played for England in the one-day internationals against West Indies at Scarborough and Edgbaston. He did little of note. He went to Australia on a Whitbread Scholarship, but it failed to satisfy his appetite for the game. Then the Australians, under Greg Chappell, arrived in England.

Botham was picked for the M.C.C. in their match against the Australians at Lord's, but he had one of his petulant fits of bowling and had limited opportunity with the bat. He was named in the squad for the one-day internationals, but he did not play in any of the matches, and he was not in the England side for the first two Tests. An injury to Chris Old, however, gave him his chance at Trent Bridge. His first spell of bowling was unproductive, but in mid-afternoon, with Australia at 131 for 2, he was brought back. His first ball was short, and Greg Chappell, intending a drive, edged the ball into his stumps. In the space of thirty-four deliveries, Botham took 4 for 13 and finished with 5 for 74. The most remarkable Test career in recent history had begun.

In the next match, at Headingley, he took 5 for 21 and then he was injured and out for the rest of the season. That winter an England side, minus their Packer players, toured Pakistan and New Zealand. Botham did not play in the Tests in Pakistan, but in the second Test in New Zealand, at Christchurch, he hit 103 with a six and 12 fours and followed it with 5 for 73 and 3 for 38. He had equalled Greig's record of scoring a hundred and taking five wickets in an innings of a Test match.

At a launching party some months after the tour ended, John Lever, the Essex pace bowler, forwarded the opinion of Botham that, 'This bloke will rewrite all the record books. I have never known anyone so confident of his own ability.' Botham began to rewrite the record books that summer.

A weak Pakistan team were England's opponents in the first part of the season. Botham hit 100 in the first Test, at Edgbaston, and followed this with 108 (his hundred off 104 balls) at Lord's, where he established a record with his 8 for 34 in the second innings.

In the second half of the summer, the New Zealanders were equally devastated by his bowling so that, after only eleven Test matches, he had taken five wickets or more in an innings eight times and scored three centuries.

England retained the 'Ashes' in Australia and when India were the visitors to England in 1979 there were more records. At Lord's, he had Gavaskar taken at slip by Brearley in the second innings to reach a hundred wickets in Test cricket a little over two years after his debut. At Headingley, he hit 99 before lunch on the fourth day of a rain-ruined Test. He had been 9 not out overnight and reached his hundred with a six off Kapil Dev. His hundred took only 121 balls, and his 137 came off 152 balls with 5 sixes and 16 fours. The Test will be recalled for nothing else but that innings of stunning brilliance. At The Oval, he completed the 'double' in what was his twenty-first Test. He had beaten Mankad's record by two Test matches. He was now a national institution.

The disastrous mini-series against Australia was lightened only by Botham's magnificent bowling and by his thrilling century at Melbourne. From there, England went to Bombay for the Golden Jubilee Test. Botham hit 114 and took 6 for 58 and 7 for 48. He had become the first to score a century and take ten or more wickets in a Test, and the first to score a hundred and take five wickets in an innings on three occasions. He was named as captain of England for the forthcoming series against West Indies. This was to be the first passage of woe in what had been a career of unabated triumph.

Botham's cricket has always been a physical expression of his strength and joy. It is an uninhibited display of a man's delight in the gifts with which he has been endowed. The size of the man, as with Grace, had to be large, for his every gesture is in the grand manner. The unquestioning belief in his own physical ability creates a massive response to any situation or crisis; it does not lead to critical analysis. Peter Roebuck insists that once, in a game at Oxford, Botham was caught at long-off off the last ball of the match in an attempt to get the 17 that Somerset needed off that ball to win. More significantly, it was rumoured recently that when a young, aspiring England fast bowler was having trouble with his run-up and approached Botham for advice, the reply he received was 'Just run up and bowl, sunshine.' It sounds callous, and it is unthinking, but it is what the man himself does.

Exuberance and self-belief are not the only qualities needed to captain a side, and some of the very best of cricketers have been the worst of captains, unable to understand that others are incapable of the heights that they themselves can reach. At schoolboy level, the best player is inevitably the captain, and often his response to the position is to want to bat and to bowl all the time because, justifiably, he thinks he can do those things better than anyone else. In essence, there has always remained something of the schoolboy in Ian Botham, and his most endearing qualities are not necessarily those most suited to captaincy. His twelve Test matches as England's captain marked a very low point in his career, both in terms of leadership and in his own performances.

Ten Tests against the West Indies, the second five of which were played in the Caribbean amid political debate about links with South Africa and overshadowed by the death of Ken Barrington, would have tried any captain; and it is noticeable that the most successful England captains, and cricketers, of recent years are those who avoided playing against the West Indies.

When Kim Hughes brought the 1981 Australians to England, Botham was still in charge. He batted number seven in the first Test, used himself as second change bowler, and England lost a Test that they should have won. In the second Test, at Lord's, English cricket seemed to have reached the very depths. There was neither guidance nor policy in the field; simply angry and empty gestures. Botham was twice out for nought. He left the field in the second innings gesticulating angrily, seeming to indicate that his failure had been wished upon him. He stormed to the selectors and resigned the captaincy.

There was some justification in his anger. Some in the media who had

Ian Botham. The most dynamic force in modern cricket. A man of mighty gesture.

urged that he be made captain had since stated that it was nonsense that he should ever have been considered suitable. His size and weight, previously symbols of his strength and power, had now become reasons for his failure. His instinctive zest for the game and his innate ability which had excited by their amateur romance were ignored as it became publicised that he did not practise enough. His capacity for drinking well and eating heartily, formerly traits of character that were accepted gleefully as being English and manly, were now considered as reasons for lack of form and fitness.

The hero had been toppled from his pedestal, but his return to the summit was rapid, dramatic and quite one of the most brilliant things ever seen in Test cricket.

Brearley returned to take over the England captaincy. A man of intelligence if very limited ability as a player, Brearley views cricket like a game of chess. He is the arch strategist, and he is also a man capable of drawing the very best from Botham. In the third Test, at Headingley, Botham took 6 for 95, but Australia made 401. He hit an exciting and responsible 50, but England were out for 174 and forced to follow-on. By mid-afternoon on the Monday, England were 135 for 7 and sinking fast. Botham then played one of the very greatest innings that the game has seen. He played simply, mightily and without inhibition. He lifted on his toes and crashed the ball through the off side. He advanced down the wicket and drove Alderman high and majestic for six. He and Dilley added 117 in 80 minutes. He and Old put on 67 in 35. Botham's hundred came off 87 balls. He equalled Gregory's record of scoring a hundred and taking five wickets in an innings of an 'Ashes' Test. He finished with 149 not out, and suddenly, and unexpectedly, Australia had to bat again. On the last day, they folded before an inspired spell of bowling by Willis, and England won by 18 runs.

At Edgbaston, Botham disappointed with the bat, and Australia needed only 151 to win. On the Sunday afternoon, with the crowd baying for blood, he took 5 wickets for 1 run in 28 balls, and England won by 29 runs.

In the fifth Test, at Old Trafford, England led by 101 on the first innings, Botham 3 for 28, but Australia fought back and had the home side at 104 for 5 in their second innings. Botham hit 118 in just over two hours off 102 balls. He reached his century off 86 deliveries, and his innings contained 6 sixes, on occasions swatting at Lillee's bouncer and sending it skying over fine leg into the crowd.

In the last Test, at The Oval, he had match figures of 10 for 253 and reached two hundred wickets in Test cricket. It was his forty-first Test. The agonies of Lord's and of the West Indies had quickly been forgotten.

The next time he played for England was in Bombay a few months later when he became the third cricketer in Test history to complete the 'double' of 2,000 runs and 200 wickets. It was a miserable series, with one faction planning their trip to South Africa for the Breweries' side, but Botham excelled. When India came to England in 1982 he celebrated his fiftieth Test with his tenth century. He followed this with 208 off 226 balls in just over four and a half hours at The Oval. He hit 4 sixes and 19 fours. He was out playing the reverse sweep. He averaged 134·33 for the series.

He thrived with the ball against Pakistan and whenever England did not win, as in the series against Australia the following winter, the blame was usually attached to Botham's failure to carry the side on his back. His every action was news, and his relationship with sections of the press became very strained. There were those who thought that his attitude and his lack of commitment to practice were irresponsible, and when he was out for 8 in the first innings of the Lord's Test against New Zealand in 1983 he gestured at the press box as if its incumbents were responsible for his failure. When he scored 61 in the second innings he offered an exaggerated bow in the same direction. His 103 at Trent Bridge did little to lessen the tension. He performed well in New Zealand and Pakistan, but defeat and accusations of scandalous behaviour off the field stole the headlines in the popular press. He returned home early through injury.

He played nobly against West Indies, but England were destroyed. In his seventy-second Test, at The Oval in 1984, he bowled a furious spell during which he had Dujon taken at slip. This gave him his three hundredth Test wicket and made him the first man to acheive the Test 'double' of 300 wickets and 3,000 runs.

He played with a lack of discipline and dignity in the Test against Sri Lanka, bowled off-breaks and still finished with 6 for 90. He asked to be excused from the England tour of India. Gower's side played well, and won. There were mutterings that the team was better without Botham, that he was a disrupting influence. It seemed that people were happy to ignore the 4,159 Test runs, 312 Test wickets and 84 Test catches as if they were of no import. In truth, his substitute, Chris Cowdrey, a most likeable and enthusiastic young man, was good enough for Test cricket as neither a batsman nor a bowler.

His hunting, shooting and fishing; his fast cars; his aeroplane; his brushes with the law and with the authorities of cricket; his escapades with Scunthorpe United and Yeovil Town; his extravagant social behaviour; his indication that he might become a film star as well as a cricketer; the claims of his one-time manager Tim Hudson that he was bigger than the game; his choice of clothes and his hair style; all these things tended to occupy more lines in the newspapers than his achievements on the field. They were coupled with intimations that his performances for Somerset were mediocre, that he was overweight, out of condition and out of breath, that he had lost the ability to bowl the outswinger and that his aversion to too much net practice would see the decline of his batting now that he was growing older.

He did not always help his own cause. At the Silk Cut Challenge at Arundel, 1985, for appearing at which he was paid a considerable sum of money, he refused to wear the sponsor's clothing, a discreet and attractive sweater with one purple band at the neck, insisting that he wore his 'Hudson's Heroes' equipment instead. In the end he wore neither, and he lost some friends. Perhaps his greatest failing is that he has never been able to distinguish between friend and sycophant; between wise adviser and self-seeking exploiter.

He excites opposite reactions among followers of the game. His every appearance is greeted by the greatest of roars because it is certain that something is about to happen, that it will be unconventional and that it will be fun. Some would press him into a position as a leader of the people, but he is far removed from that. He is an individual, almost an eccentric, a rebel who paradoxically clings to traditional loyalties.

His personality can be magnetic. One may have been outraged by a recent action or statement and then meet him at a reception wearing his black leather trousers and Hudson-striped jacket, tie and hat and be drawn towards him, and a comment on his costume will bring the reply that whatever your figure and your weight, he is sure that you can be fitted and will look splendid in the same clothes. And he is not just being polite.

Somerset finished bottom of the county championship in 1985 and, amid growing pressure, Botham relinquished the captaincy. His own contribution to the season had been to score more than a thousand runs and average over 100 in the championship. He also hit 80 sixes during the season and established a phenomenal record. In gloomy light at Edgbaston, on 26 July, he reached a hundred off 50 balls in 49 minutes. He finished with 138 not out in 65 minutes with 12 sixes and 13 fours.

In the fifth Test match, also at Edgbaston, he came to the wicket when England already had 572 runs on the board. He hit two of the first three balls he received, from McDermott, into the crowd for six. His batting nearly thwarted Australia at Lord's, and his outswinger did not seem to have deserted him, for he took 31 wickets in the series. He also made eight catches, two of them in the slips in The Oval Test which defy description for their anticipation and athleticism.

At the end of the season he walked from John o' Groats to Land's End in aid of leukaemia research. He walked at a pace each day which would have made many wilt, and he ate and drank heartily in the evening which certainly made many wilt. In some quarters his walk was seen as self-publicity, but he hardly needed any more publicity than he was already receiving. He did it because he was passionate about a cause, and because he does nothing in small measures. It was a massive gesture by a big man.

Like nearly all others in the England side, he failed in the West Indies in 1986, and again the tour was shadowed by controversy and innuendo. Botham was crucified by a section of the press, and with one newspaper he continued a running battle. The result was a suspension that kept him out of cricket for June and July. Before it began he hit the last two balls of a John Player League match for six to win the game for Somerset, and he returned with a blazing Sunday innings against Northamptonshire at Wellingborough. It was said that he was bowling badly, at half-pace, and that he should not be recalled to the England side.

England, however, had lost badly to India, and they were one down to New Zealand, and there was not a batsman in the side who was playing with confidence or consistency. Ian Botham was chosen for The Oval Test, the last of the summer. The match was to be ruined by rain, but Botham was to make it memorable. It was his eighty-fifth Test.

Gatting won the toss and asked New Zealand to bat. They had reached 17 when Botham was brought into the attack. As he was called up there was a bustle in the crowd which broke into cheering. His first delivery was medium pace and a little short, but Edgar, as if mesmerised, steered it straight to Gooch at slip where it was caught at the second attempt. That wicket brought him level with Dennis Lillee as the leading wicket-taker in Test history. There is a hypnotic quality in the man; he casts spells on his opponents.

He could have beaten Lillee's record next ball, but Emburey missed a difficult low chance at slip. Jeff Crowe was the fortunate batsman, but a few minutes later Botham hurried one through to trap him leg before. He stood with legs apart, raised his arms high, clenched his fists and exulted.

On the Monday morning, England needed quick runs to have any hope of victory. Botham hit 59 off 36 balls in 55 minutes. He hit 4 sixes and 4 fours, and in one over from Derek Stirling he equalled the record in Test cricket by taking 24 from the over. Lever's prophecy had come true: 'The bloke has rewritten all the record books.'

He remains a figure of controversy, but no cricketer since W.G. Grace has been such a national figure. His likeness is instantly recognised by those who have never been to a match nor shown any interest in the game. Books about him grow week by week – Farmer, Doust, Eagar and Arlott, Keating – in the perpetual search for the man or the legend. Perhaps we are too close to the events to give a true and a balanced assessment, but the figures themselves are staggering.

Eventually, only history can decide whether Botham will be ranked above or alongside Grace or Sobers. Whether, like Grace, he will be forgiven his excesses is also a decision that will be made in the passage of time.